THE ESSENCE OF

HERMÈS

UNFOLDED

UNOFFICIAL & UNAUTHORIZED

CON

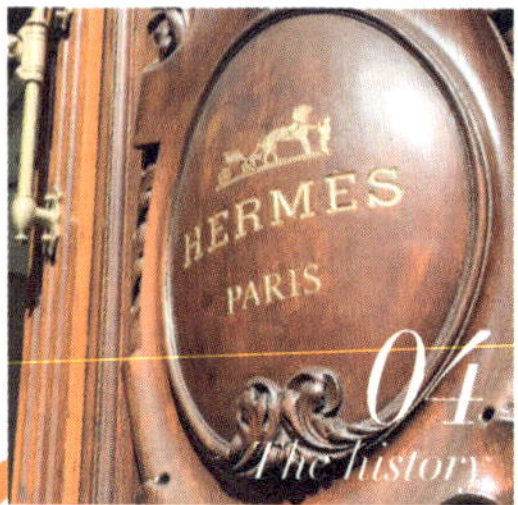

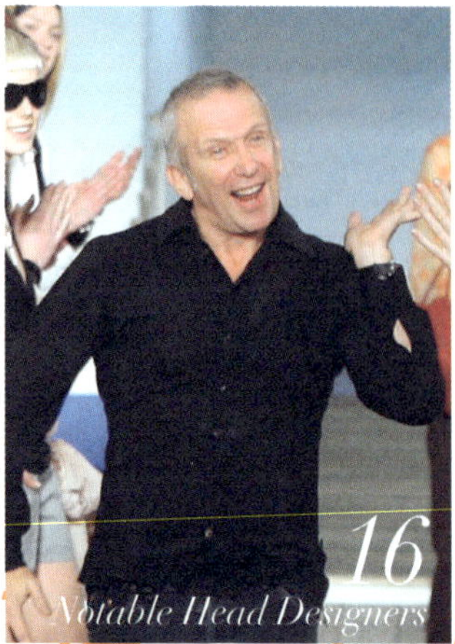

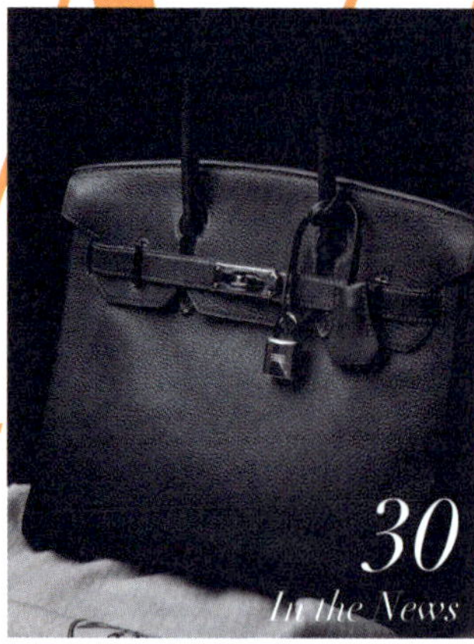

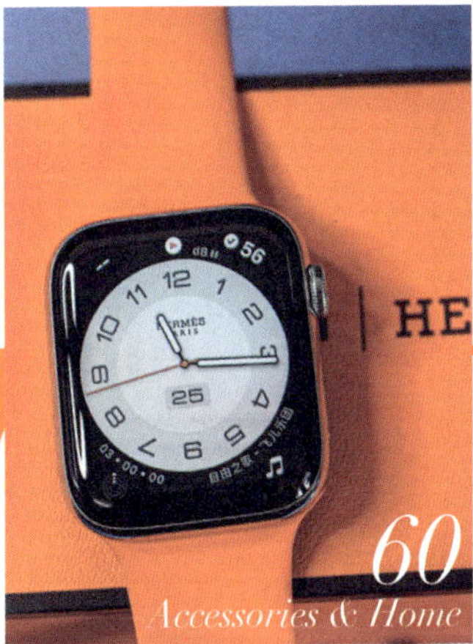
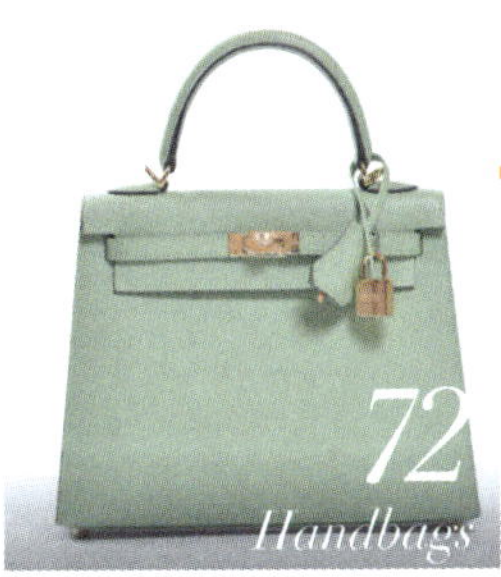
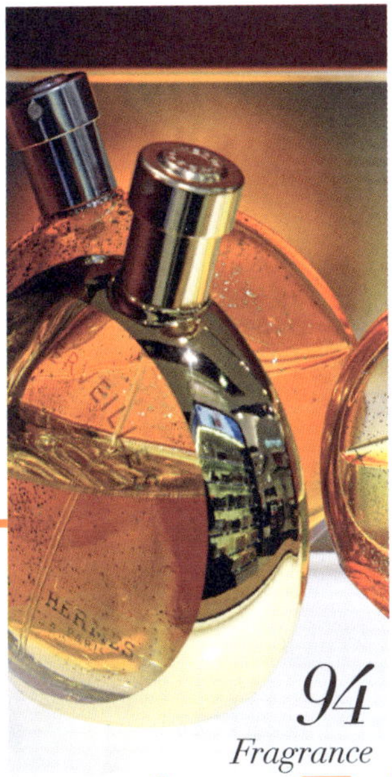
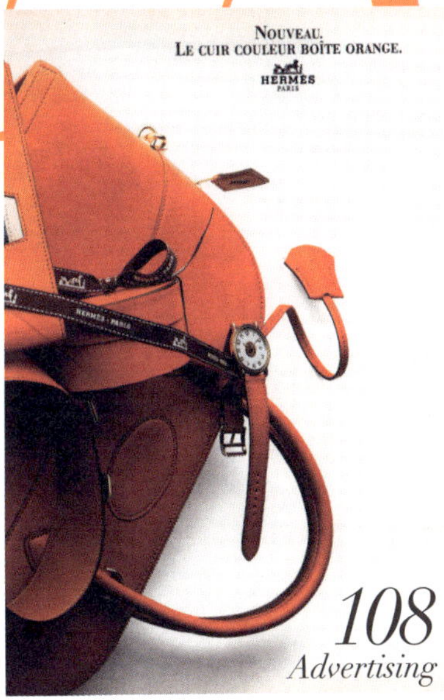
NOUVEAU.
LE CUIR COULEUR BOÎTE ORANGE.
HERMÈS
PARIS
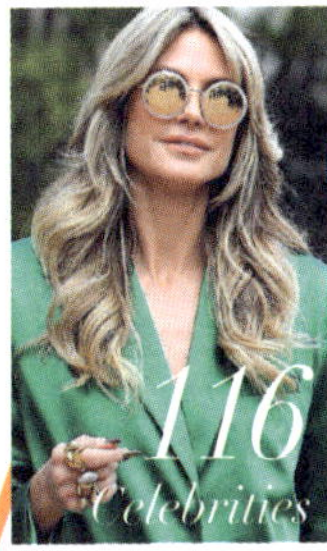
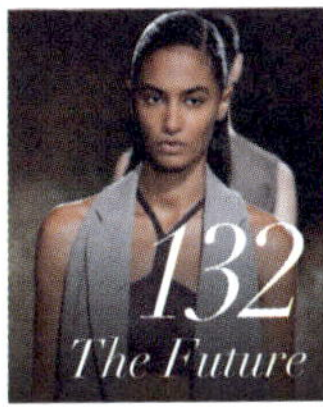

1

The Beginning of HERMÈS

The History

Even people who aren't into luxury goods know that a Hermès Birkin handbag is a very special and coveted item. Not to mention that it's about as expensive as a small compact car, or even a Rolls Royce in some cases. What's even more special is the fact that Hermès is one of the oldest luxury goods makers still around today, created 187 years ago in 1837. They have fashion for both women and men, home goods, equestrian items, fragrances, watches, jewelry, and even makeup now. And, of course, the high-end handbags, such as the Birkin and the Kelly bag.

This French luxury design house was established by Thierry Hermès, who was born in Germany. His mother was German while his father was French. When Thierry grew up, he established a shop in Paris that made harnesses for horse carriages. That's why the logo for the brand is a picture of a horse-drawn carriage. The harnesses were so high end and beautiful that only the most upper-class society of Paris could afford them. It definitely set the bar for the kind of luxury goods that Hermès still makes to this day. Expensive. Exclusive. Posh. Thierry had a son named Charles-Émile, who took over management of the brand in 1880. He moved the headquarters to the famous 24 Rue du Faubourg Saint-Honore, where it's still located today. Charles-Émile also had two sons, Thierry's grandsons, who became part of the business. Adolphe and Émile-Maurice eventually took leadership of the company as they began to sell more saddles and other accessories for equestrians horse owners.

In 1900, one of their signature products was a bag called the Haut à Courroies, which allowed a rider to carry different types of saddles with them. The saddles and accessories the company created were very sought after. They were sold all over the world to royalty, and eventually, in 1918, they started making clothing. One of the company's first designs was a leather golf jacket for the Prince of Wales, Edward. The company was well on its way to offering diverse types of products, not just products for horse owners. More accessories and other clothing types soon followed as Émile-Maurice ran the brand.

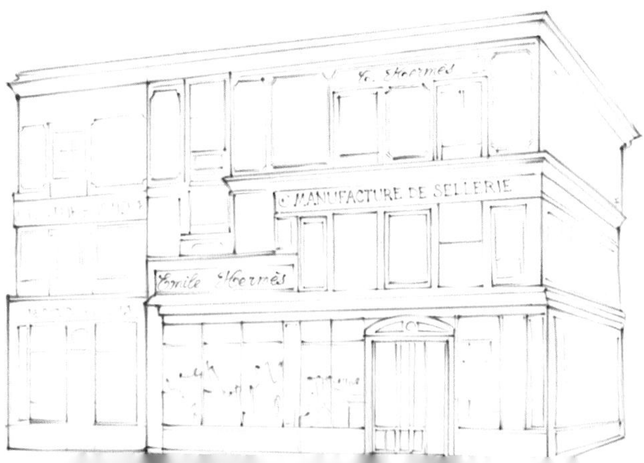

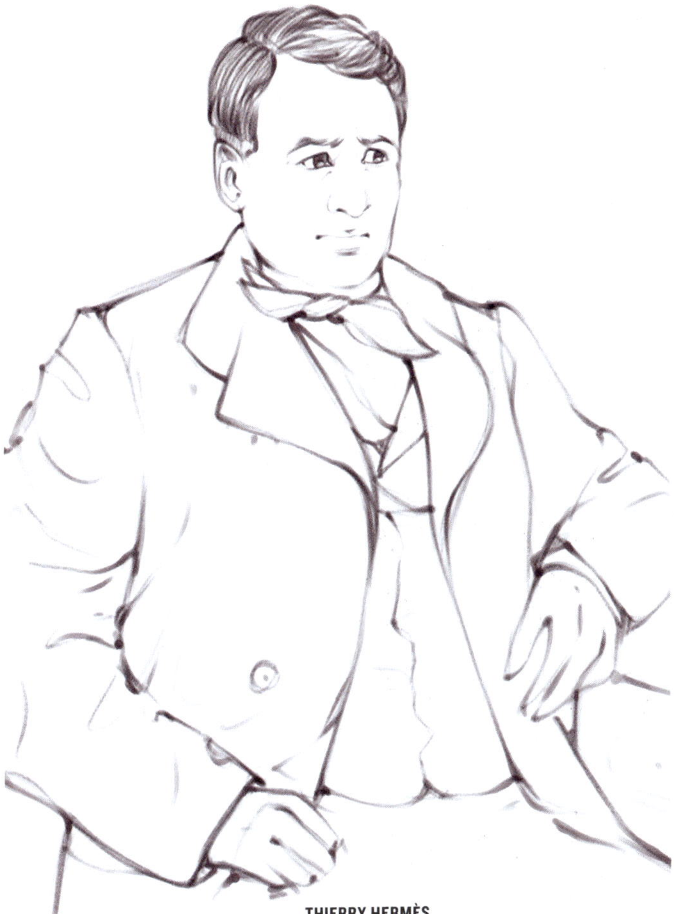

THIERRY HERMÈS

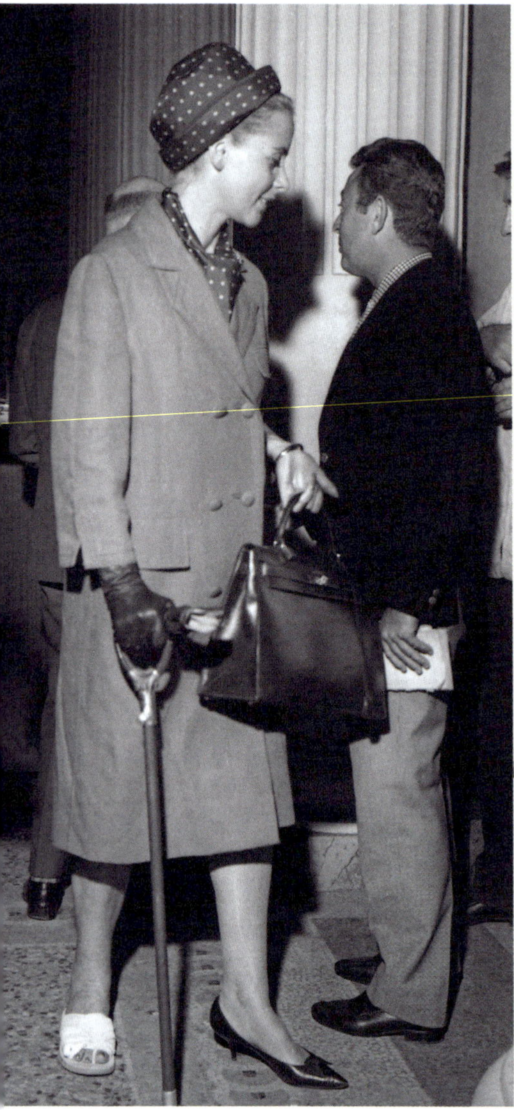

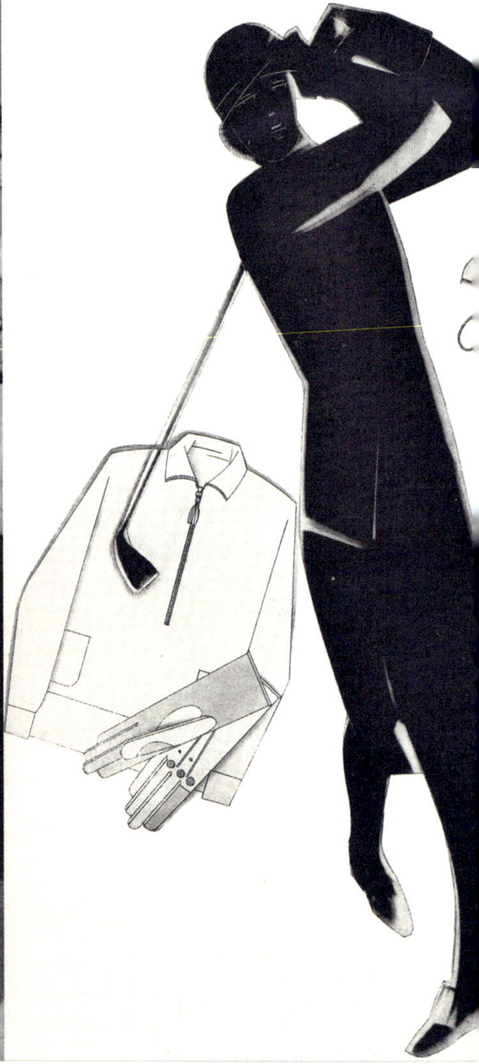

KELLY

Princess Grace of Monaco with the Kelly bag. This photo, taken in 1963, shows Princess Grace using crutches due to a foot injury.

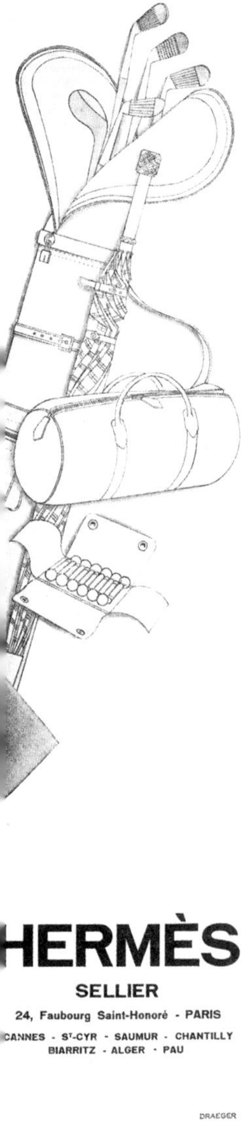

In 1922, Émile-Maurice created the first handbag for the brand, since his wife complained that she couldn't find one that she liked. This was the start of what Hermès is mostly known for in pop culture: their high-end handbags.

During the next era, in the 1930s, two of Hermès' most iconic items were created. One was the Kelly bag, named after Princess Grace Kelly of Monaco. It was originally called Sac à dépêches; it wasn't named for the princess officially until 1977, although she did carry it in the 50s when she was pregnant, holding the bag over her stomach when she was out in public. She was photographed with it many times, which is why the company honored her by naming it the Kelly bag.

The other popular item that came out in the 30s was the Hermès scarf. It was a square-shaped scarf that made its debut in 1937. These scarves, which are still a popular part of the luxury house today, are gorgeous, are made of silk, and have lots of different colors and patterns on them. As a fashion accessory, everyone wanted to have one at the time and over the years. It's truly an iconic style to own that can be worn in numerous ways. The popularity of the scarf has gone up and down, but it's still something that the luxury house releases new designs of every year. People collect them and hand them down through the generations.

Gradually, through those early decades, they introduced more products, such as men's silk ties, fragrances, jewelry, watches, and other luxury products that were inspired by art. Their iconic orange paper boxes were introduced in the 50s. The boxes come in a variety of sizes and are unmistakable, with their bright orange hue and brown lettering. Then, in the 60s, multiple stores were opened worldwide, with locations including Hong Kong, New York, and Switzerland.

The 80s brought on even more products, including a very popular tableware line that had plates, cups, glasses, and silverware. These were truly gorgeous French-created products that became popular wedding and shower presents. The Hermès family was still involved at every step of the expansion, and today they are one of the only luxury goods makers to be family owned. Or, at least, they are majority owned by the Hermès family. Even though Hermès is a publicly traded company, the family still owns an 80 percent stake in the company. That means they have a controlling interest in this billion-dollar brand. The other 20 percent was at one time owned by luxury conglomerate Louis Vuitton Moet Hennessy, or LVMH. They own such brands as Tiffany & Co, Gucci, Sephora, Fendi, and Dior.

In 2019, Forbes Magazine ranked Hermès number 33 on their "World's Most Valuable Brands" list, with sales reaching $13 billion in 2023. They have at least 14 different product lines, with the most popular ones being leather goods, clothes, scarves, and other items, such as housewares and jewelry. To have something made by Hermès is to own a piece of history. Their items are like works of art, with almost 200 years of fine French craftsmanship behind them.

GRADUALLY, TH

THOSE EARLY

THEY INTRODU

PRODUCTS SUC

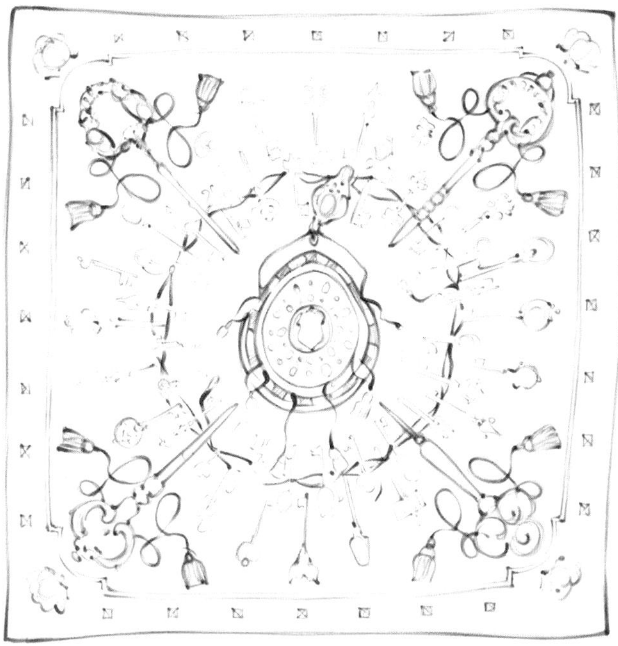

PAPER BOXES W

DUCED IN THE

ES COME IN AV

SIZES AND ARE

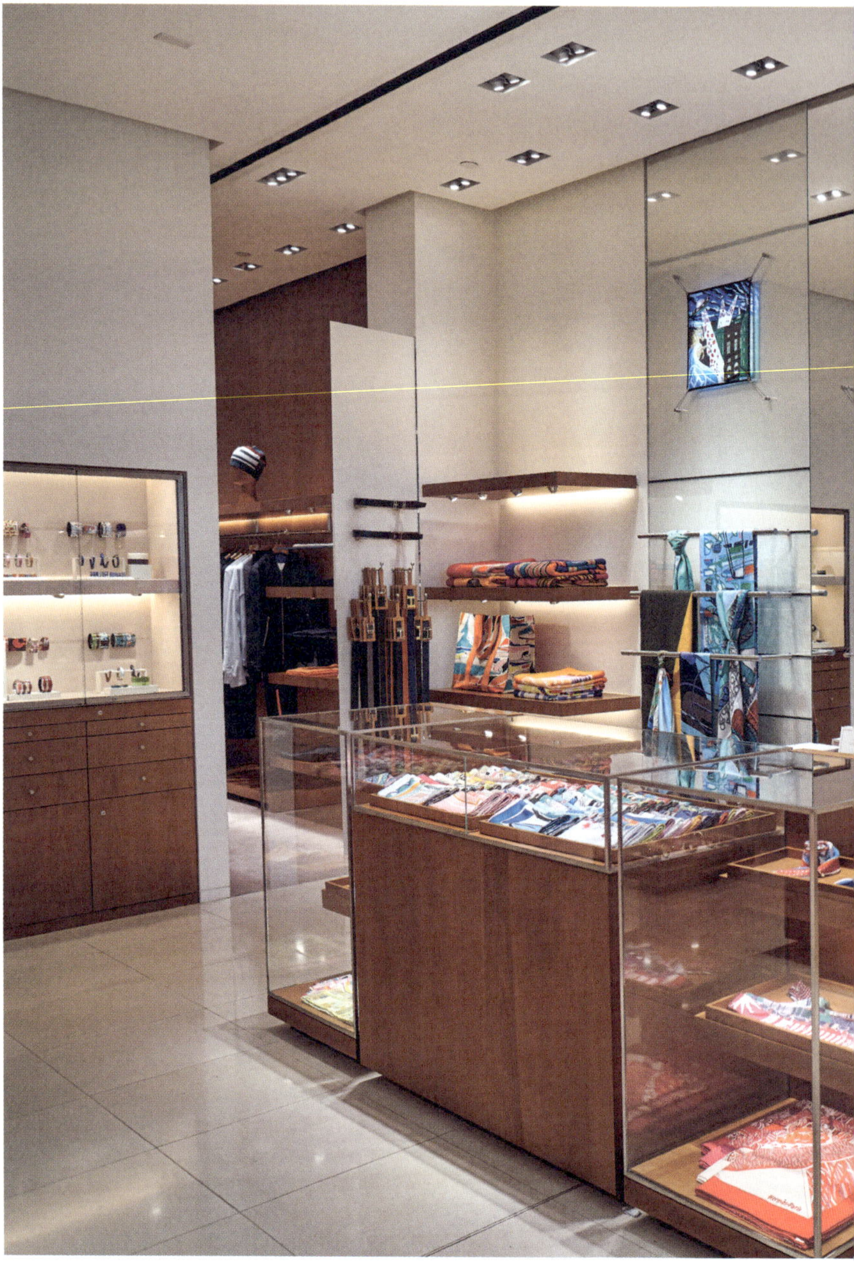

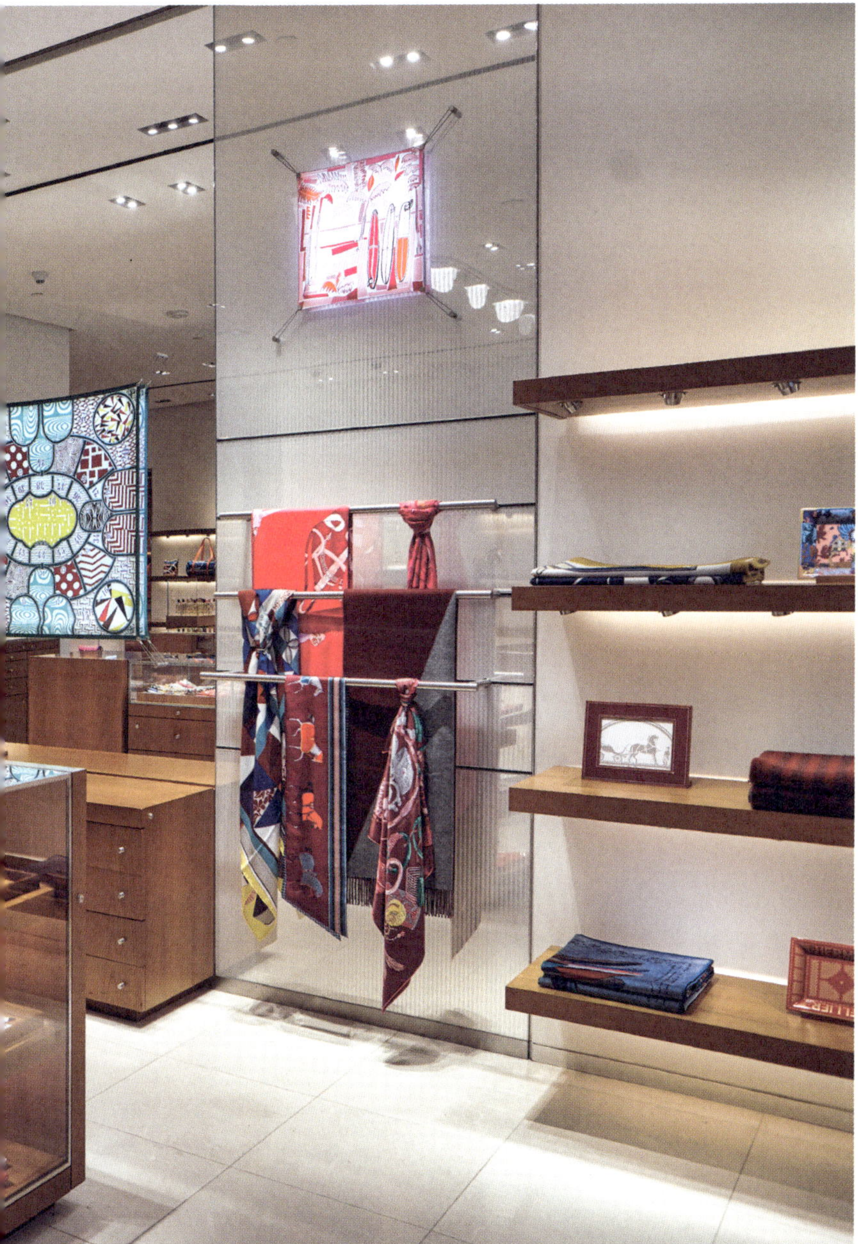

“LEATHER IS OUR HISTORY, SILK OUR HERITAGE, AND CRAFTS-MANSHIP OUR TRADITION.”

Thierry Hermès

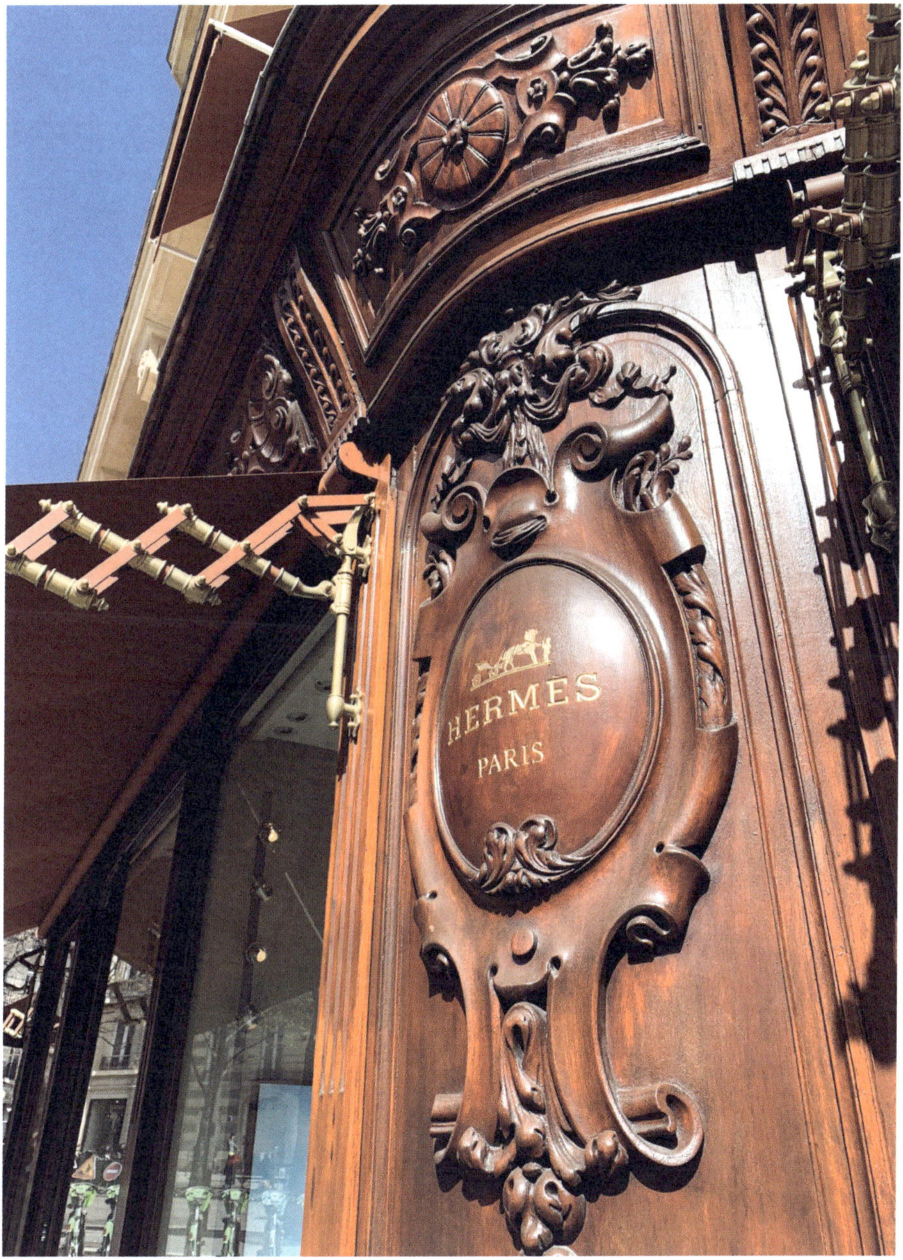
HERMES
PARIS

2

MARTIN MARGIELA, *JEAN-PAUL GAULTIER*, CHRISTOPHE LEMAIRE, *NADÈGE VANHEE -CYBULSKI*

Notable Head Designers

HERMÈS IS A UNIQUE LUXURY COMPANY because they didn't always make clothing. It's not even what they are really known for in the general public's awareness. The first women's ready-to-wear collection came out in 1967, designed by Catherine Karolyi. She was the one responsible for creating the famous "H" buckle that is still so popular today. As the head designer, she stayed with Hermès until 1980. The luxury brand has had a slew of designers since then, but here are some of the most popular people who have helmed the creative direction of the line for women's ready-to-wear in the past 27 years.

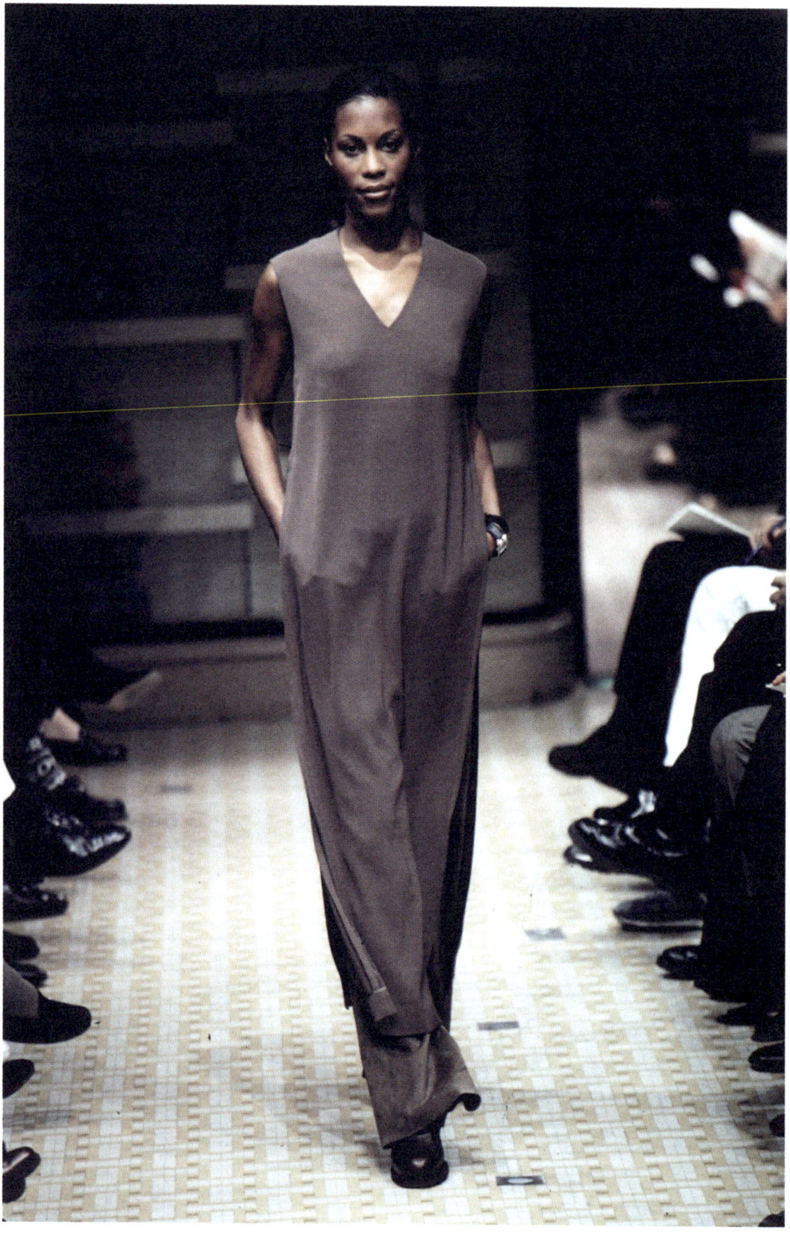

Model on the runway at Martin Margiela's first Hermès fashion show.

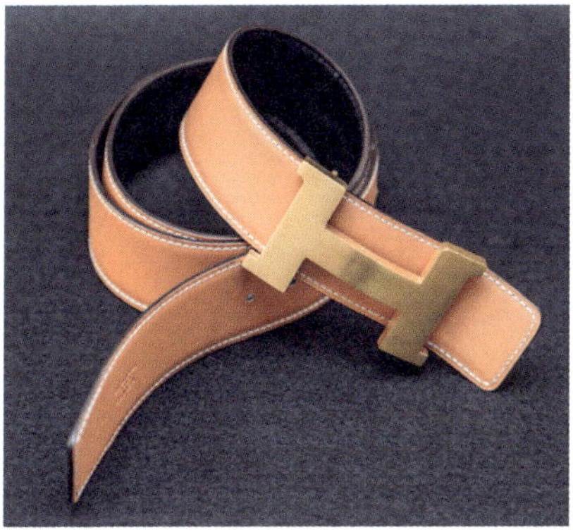

Martin Margiela

This Belgium fashion designer was the head of Hermès from 1997 to 2003. He studied at the Royal Academy of Fine Arts in Antwerp. His first major job in fashion was working as an assistant for Jean-Paul Gaultier until 1987. He left to start his own line, which he named after himself. During the time he had his eponymous label, he was offered the job as creative director of women's wear at Hermès.

The whole industry was in uproar over the fact that Martin was going to design for such a traditional and classic fashion house. His designs tended to be more avant garde, original, and cutting edge while, on the other hand, Hermès had been around since the mid-1800s, with their clothing being described as an "old money" look. Nevertheless, he managed to thrive at Hermès, designing classic looks that were based on 1920s leisure wear. The designs were very elegant but also practical for travel. One of his looks was a jacket that could be rolled up into a bag shape and carried. It was ideal for taking on trips practically anywhere in the world where one would need a light jacket. Oddly enough, when he decided to walk away from Hermès to focus exclusively on his own line, his old boss, Jean-Paul Gaultier, took over his position.

Jean-Paul Gaultier

The flamboyant French fashion designer Jean-Paul Gaultier was an extraordinary choice for Hermès to make for their new creative director. Before that, he helmed his own line, Jean-Paul Gaultier, and continued to design for that line until he retired completely in 2020. He worked for Hermès for seven years from 2003 to 2010.

Jean-Paul is known for outrageous designs that are a bit unconventional, such as corsets, striped navy blouses, and kilts. He created a very successful line of fragrances for both men and women. His reputation in the fashion industry is legendary, being called the "enfant terrible," as he displayed controversial behavior on more than one occasion. So the fact that a company as traditional, and some might say stiff or stuffy, as Hermès would want Jean-Paul was very interesting. The result was amazing. His avant-garde designs combined with the classic Hermès look were spectacular. A powerhouse of design creativity, he made revamped versions of the Kelly bag and the Birkin bag.

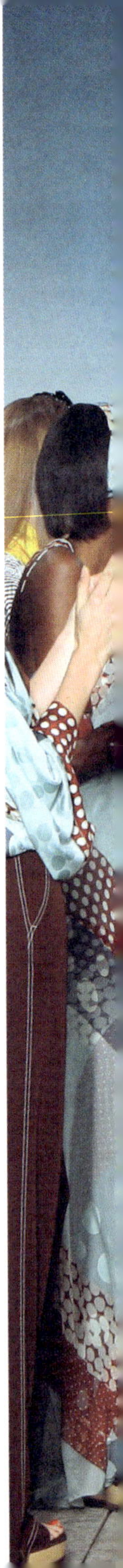

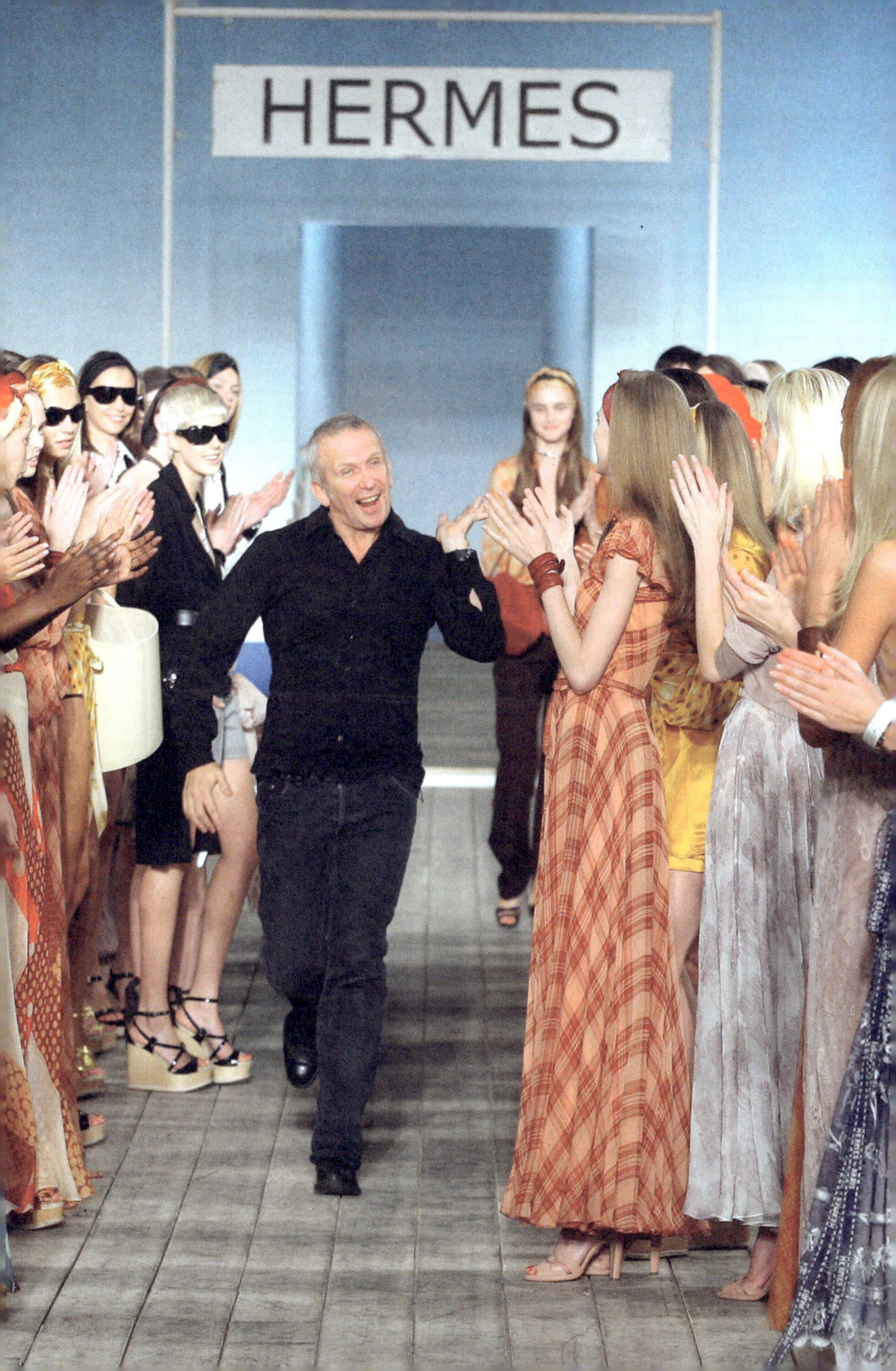
HERMES

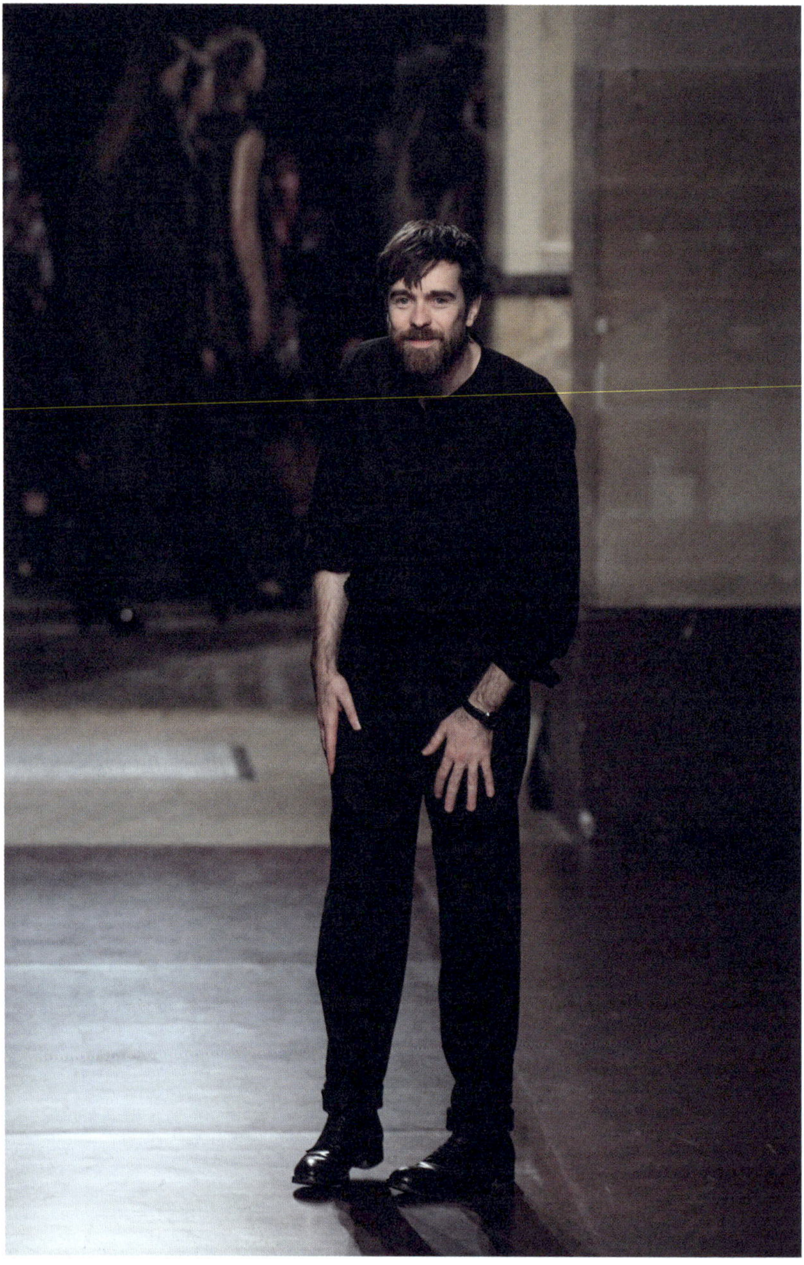

Christophe Lemaire

Christophe Lemaire took up the Hermès creative director role after Jean-Paul left on good terms. Christophe is a French designer who brought back a more understated elegance to women's ready-to-wear for the luxury fashion house. He previously worked at the brand Lacoste for 10 years, which is known for its tennis wear and sports clothing.

When he was at Hermès for those four years from 2010 to 2014, his designs were such a contrast to Jean-Paul's in their minimalism. That's not to say that they weren't successful or gorgeous, but the clothing was all about practical dressing, not flash or drama. When he was designing for Hermès, he wanted the clothing above all to be comfortable, to have functionality, and to last forever with the highest quality. His styles were truly about quiet luxury in pieces that were meant to be long-wearing staples of elegance. He decided to leave Hermès to focus on his own clothing line, which he had put on hold while he was at the luxury fashion house.

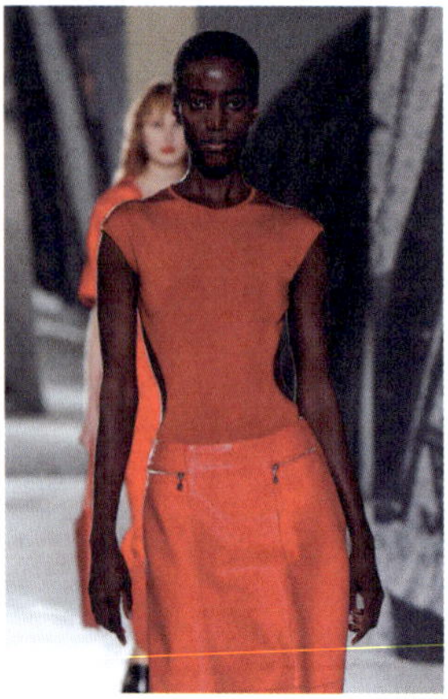

Nadège Vanhee-Cybulski

The current creative director of Hermès is Nadège Vanhee-Cybulski, who replaced Christophe in 2014. She is from Seclin, France, but also studied at the Royal Academy of Fine Arts in Antwerp, like Martin Margiela did. Her background included working for such companies as The Row and Celine as a lead designer, but Hermès was her first time as head creative director.

At 45 years old today, her work at Hermès sticks pretty close to the brand's roots. In 2015, her first collection had an equestrian theme and incorporated lots of leather along with one of the luxury house's most famous items, the silk scarf. Even though she incorporated the past, and Hermès' heritage, into the collection, she managed to put a fresh-enough take on it to be interesting. She's also the first woman to helm the Hermès brand since Catherine Karolyi left in 1980.

One of the best designs she's come up with so far for Hermès is actually a shoe. A clog. When she was in college, Nadège wore clogs a lot. So when she needed a shoe for the 2021 ready-to-wear runway show, she came up with a classic clog. People went crazy for the Hermès Cafe Clog that year. And at $1,000 bucks a pair, they are definitely a luxury clog to wear. They sold out immediately, becoming something of a status symbol. Overall, Nadège's designs for Hermès have a sort of intellectual prettiness to them. Elegantly sexy but never over the top. It will be interesting to see her continued work at such a historically esteemed and admired luxury brand.

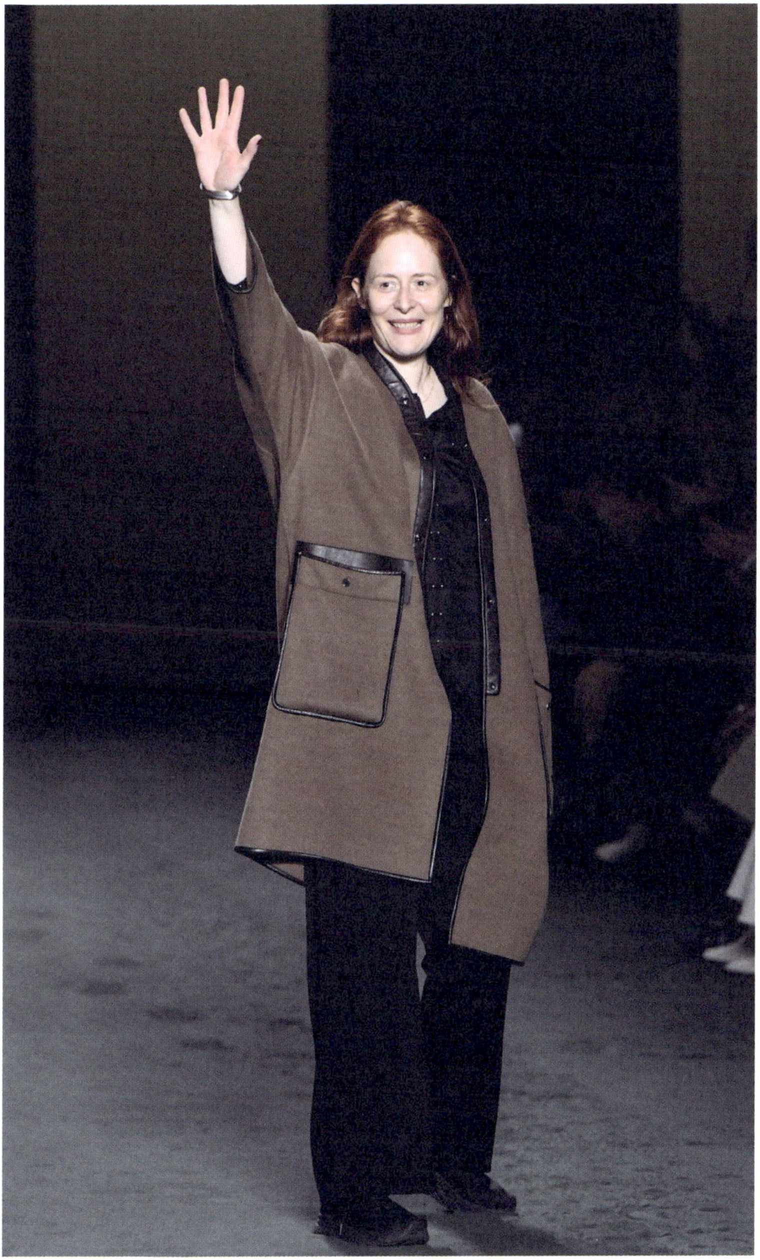

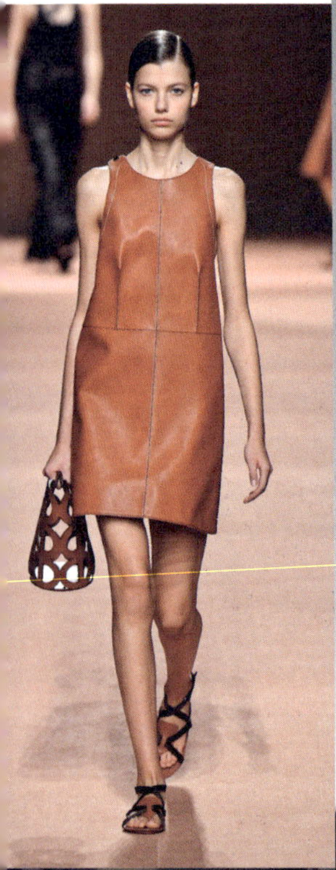

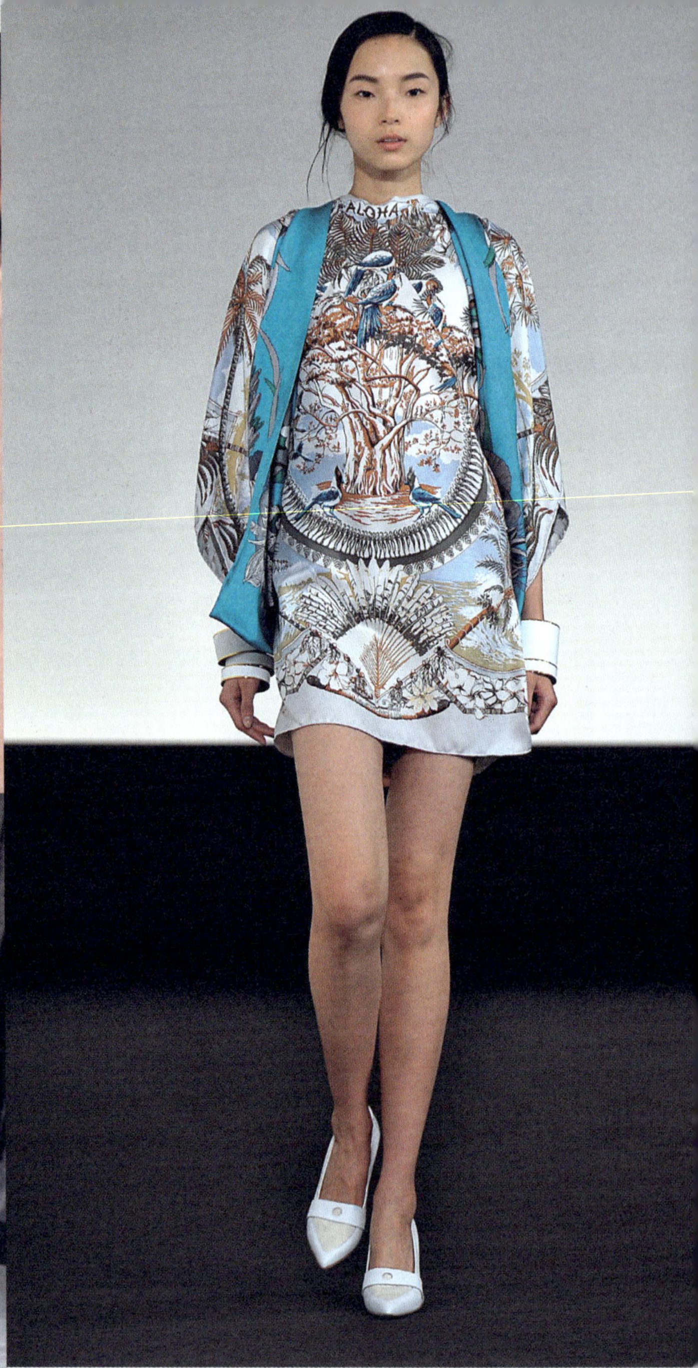
ALOHA

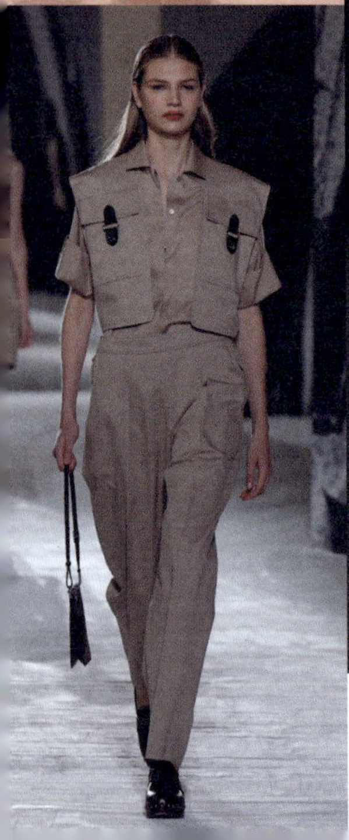

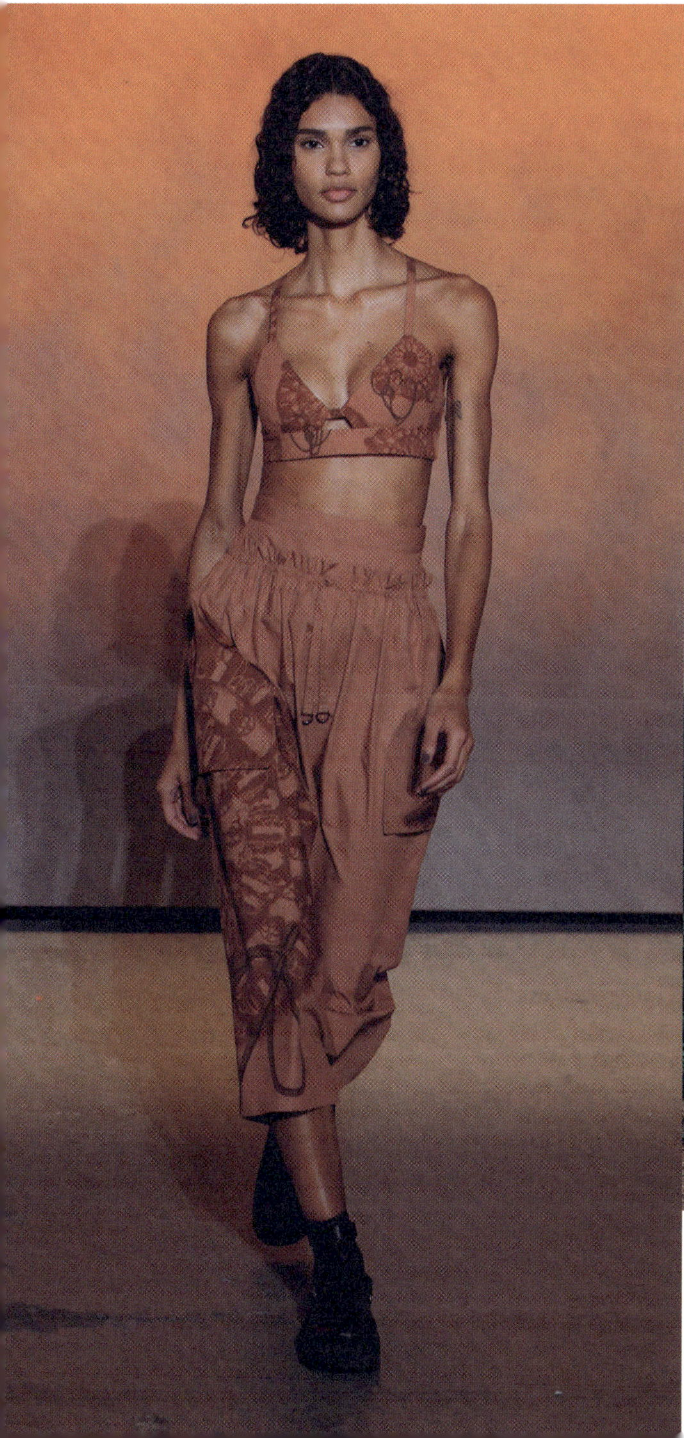

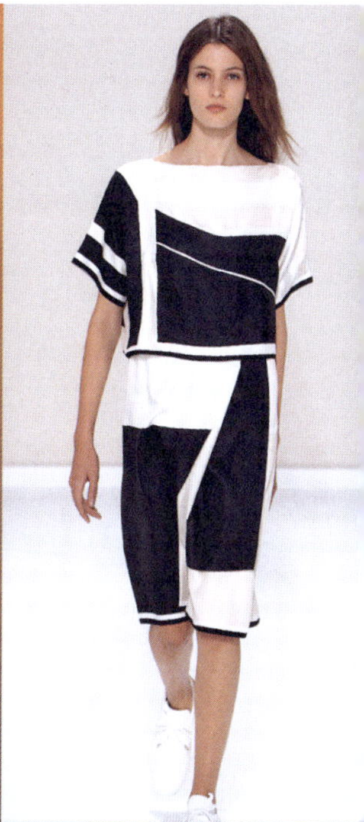

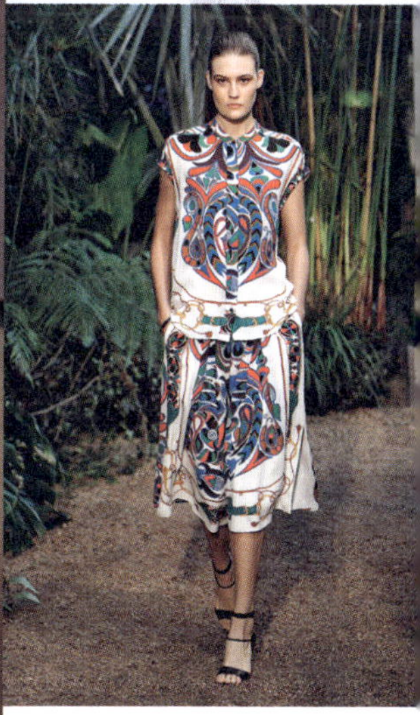

“HERMÈS IS NOT JUST ABOUT FASHION; IT’S ABOUT A LIFESTYLE, A PHILOSOPHY.”

Olivia Palermo

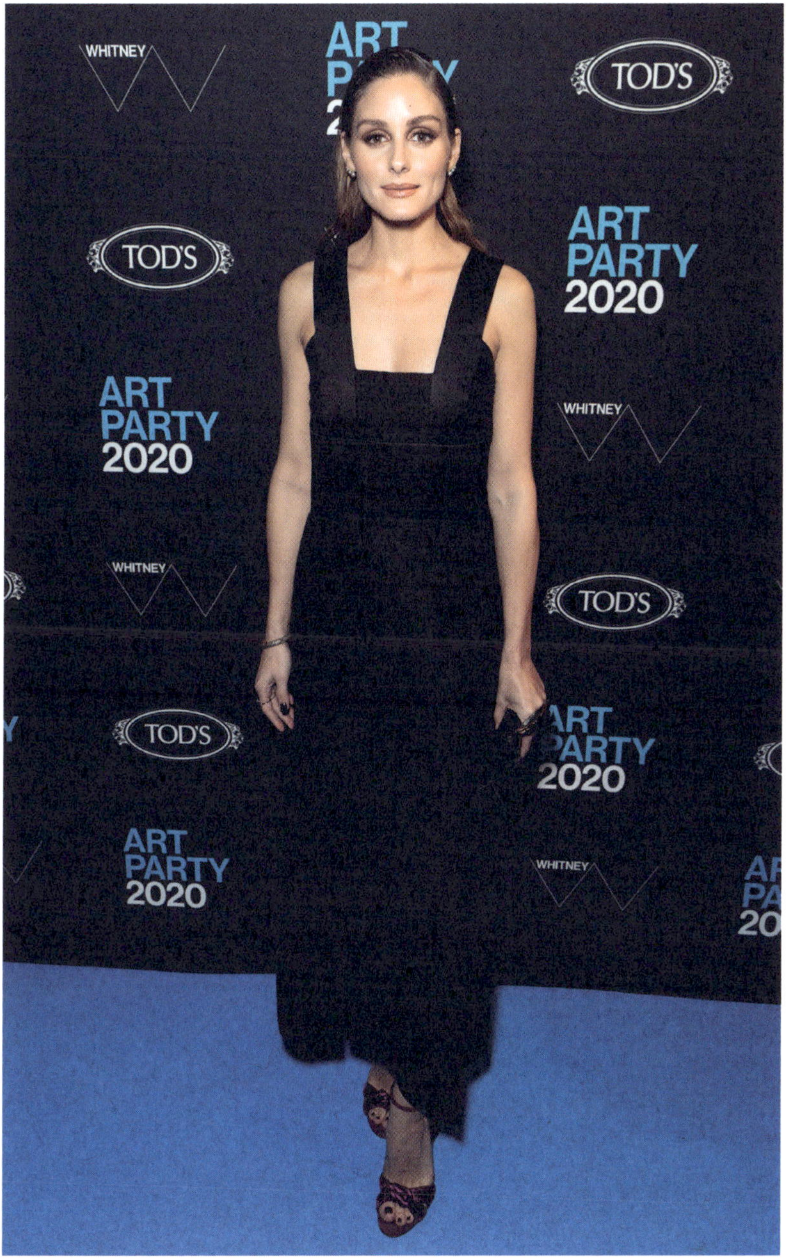
WHITNEY
TOD'S
ART
PARTY
2020

3

In the HEADLINES *with* HERMÈS

In the News

BEING IN THE NEWS, GOOD OR BAD, always brings attention to a luxury brand. When such an exclusive brand as Hermès ends up in the news, it piques everyone's attention. Since they have been around for almost 200 years, it's inevitable that things would happen within the company that make for some pretty scandalous headlines. Here are some of the most interesting news stories over the years involving this luxury goods company.

THE FIGHT BETWEEN HERMÈS *and* LVMH

Since 2001, LVMH has had a keen interest in acquiring Hermès. Although the company is still majority owned by the Hermès family, LVMH has gotten its hooks into quite a few shares of the company over the years, beginning with an acquisition of around 5 percent through subsidiaries in 2001.

Almost 10 years later, that percentage jumped to 14.2 percent, but LVMH always said that they weren't attempting a hostile takeover. Hermès wasn't buying that and "circled the wagons," so to speak, to fend them off. Just a year later, it went up to a 21 percent stake, so Hermès took legal action. The Hermès CEO, Patrick Thomas, said that LVMH acquired this higher stake in an unethical way. So the two companies have basically been fighting back and forth for years. Hermès has somehow managed to hold them off, and LVMH owns less than 2 percent of the brand today.

LVMH CEO BERNARD ARNAULT

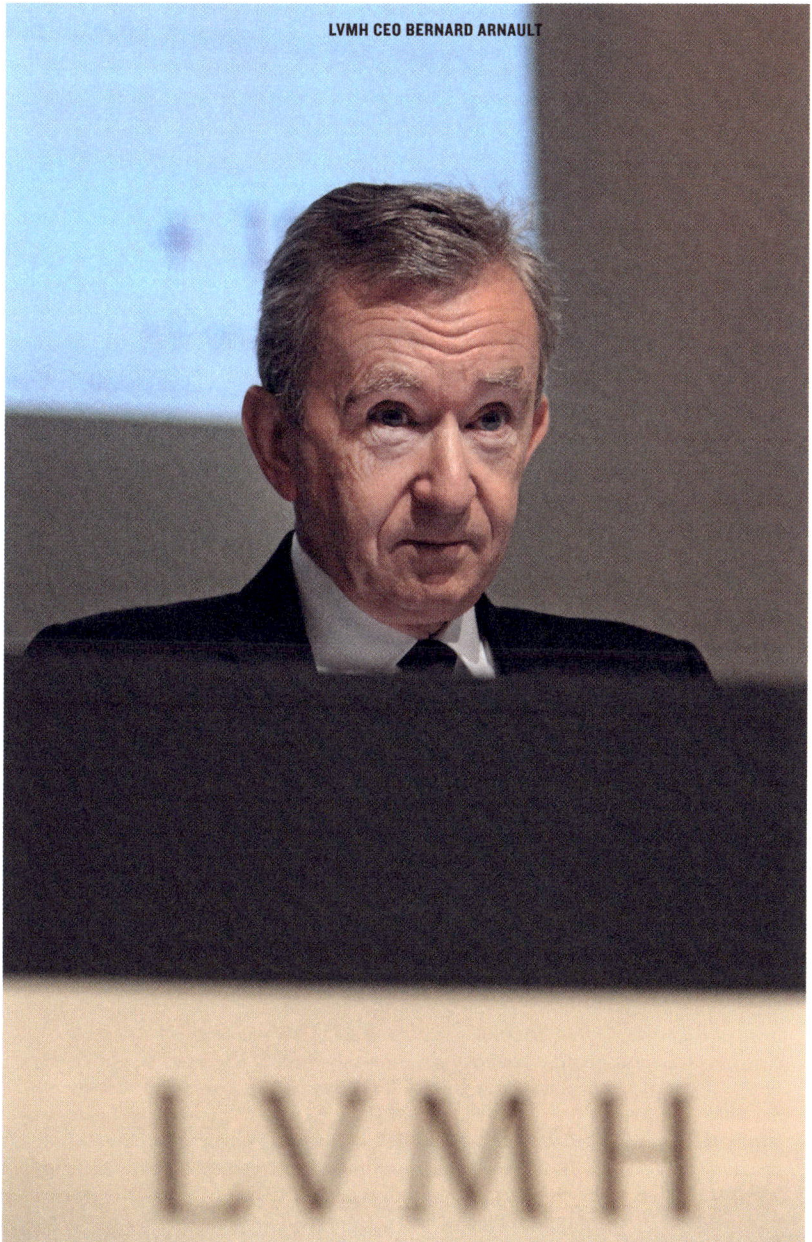

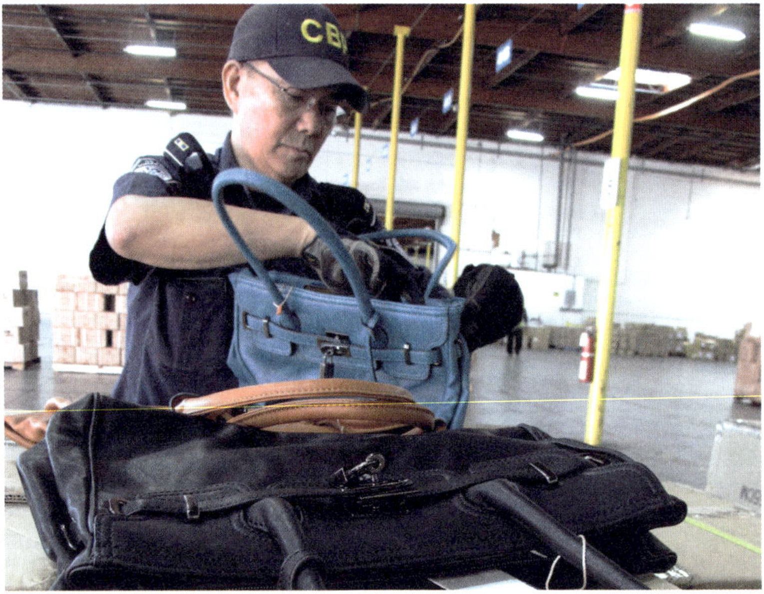

HERMÈS EMPLOYEES *in a* COUNTERFEIT RING

In a $20 million counterfeit ring bust, nine former Hermès employees were indicted in France in 2012. It involved 34 websites selling fake Hermès bags, including the Birkin and Kelly bags. There were secret workshops in Hong Kong and parts of France. Hundreds of bags were sold, with this case not being resolved until 2021, when some of the masterminds of the scam were sent to prison.

All luxury brands have issues with criminals making and selling counterfeit goods. That includes Gucci, Louis Vuitton, Dior, and Tiffany & Co. Hermès especially has problems with counterfeiters because their bags are so highly coveted and more expensive than most other luxury handbags. A basic new Birkin bag goes for between $10,000 and $12,000. That doesn't even come close to what a limited-edition one would cost, or a Birkin made with more exotic materials, such as crocodile. A crocodile Birkin can typically go for around $200,000 on the resale market. So you can see that counterfeiting gives criminals the chance to make some serious money. All luxury brands have departments that help to fight this problem, along with government organizations such as the FBI, Interpol, and US Customs and Border Protection.

HORRIBLE HERMÈS CROCODILE FARMS

Speaking of crocodiles, People for the Ethical Treatment of Animals, or PETA, spoke out about the appalling conditions that alligators and crocodiles endure while being farmed for their skin. The farms, in Texas, are used by Hermès and other luxury brands. They send the animal skins to a Hermès-owned tannery, where they are processed to be ready to be made into a number of leather goods, such as the Birkin bag, the Kelly bag, watch bands, and even a famed "H" logo belt.

PETA exposed that the animals were overcrowded and had no access to sunshine, fresh air, or clean water. In other words, these conditions were inhumane in every possible way for these poor animals. We'll spare you the more gruesome details. Needless to say, this is not great PR for Hermès, which is one of the few luxury companies that still use exotic animal skins.

Many companies have committed to not using these types of skin, including high-end brands such as Chanel, Chloe, and Burberry. PETA is constantly petitioning and campaigning to get Hermès to stop using exotic animal skins. Back in 2015, even Jane Birkin, the famous model who the Birkin bag is actually named for, implored Hermès to stop using these types of materials made from animals. It remains to be seen what Hermès will decide to do with these upscale leather goods.

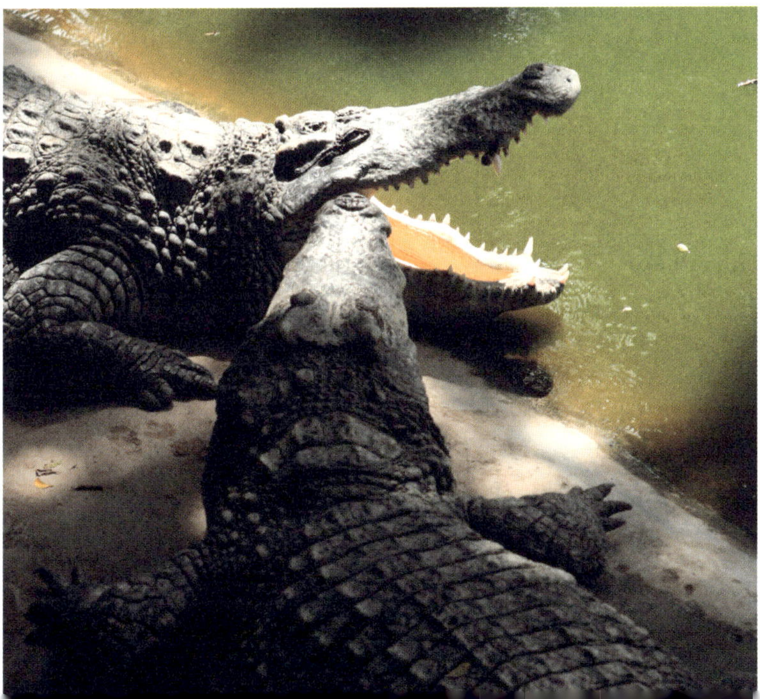

DISGRACED SENATOR GEORGE SANTOS *and* HERMÈS

George Santos, a former congressman from New York, was thrown out of Congress in December 2023. One of the reasons was that he allegedly used campaign funds to cover some personal expenses. That included going to various spas and resorts but also the purchase of luxury goods, such as the almost $5,000 he spent at a Hermès store. No one really knows exactly what he purchased, but for example, it could have been a leather and canvas bag that goes for a little under $4,000.

He was even photographed carrying a large traditional orange and brown Hermès shopping bag when he was moving into his sister's apartment. Well, at least George has some great taste, even if his financial situation is questionable.

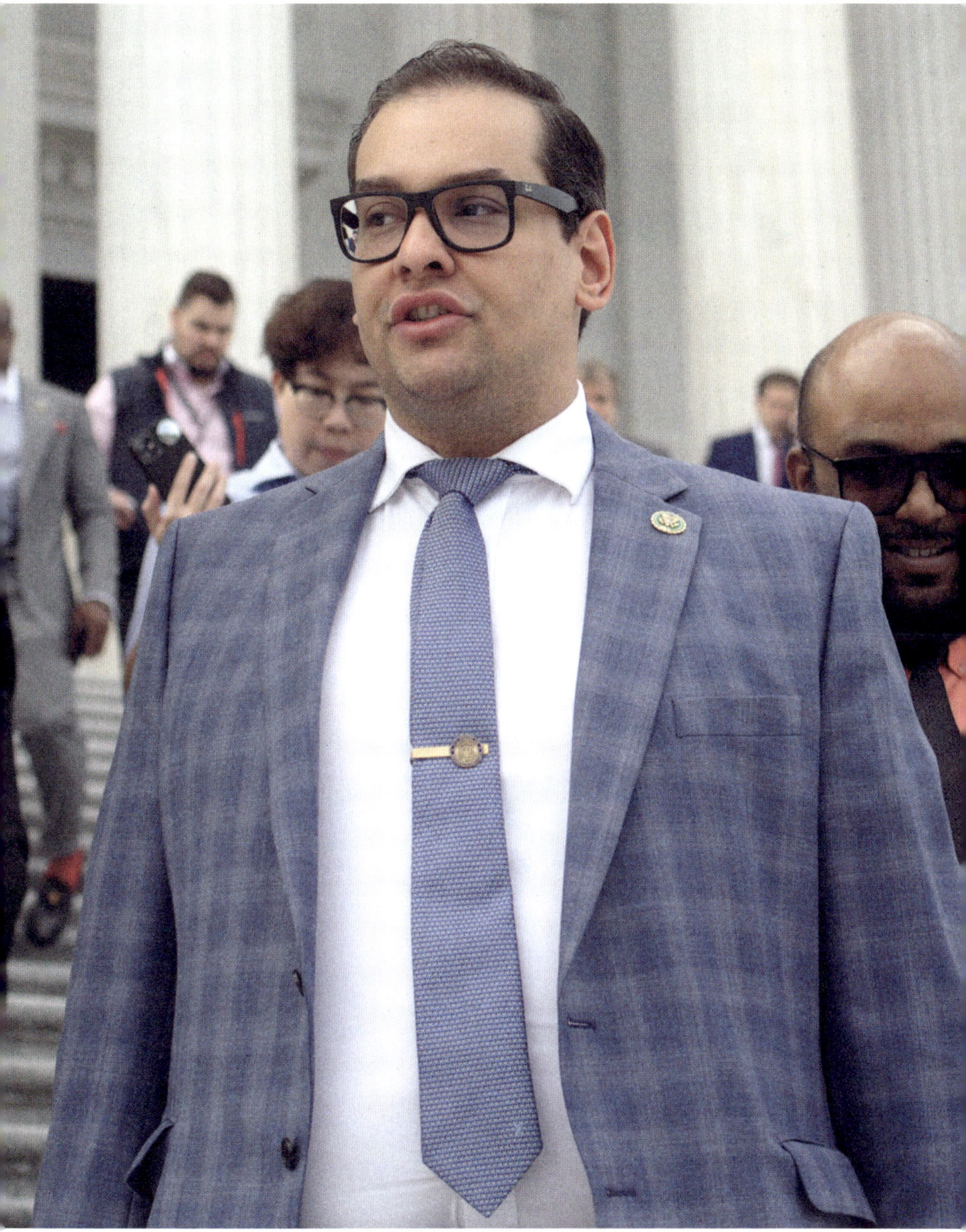

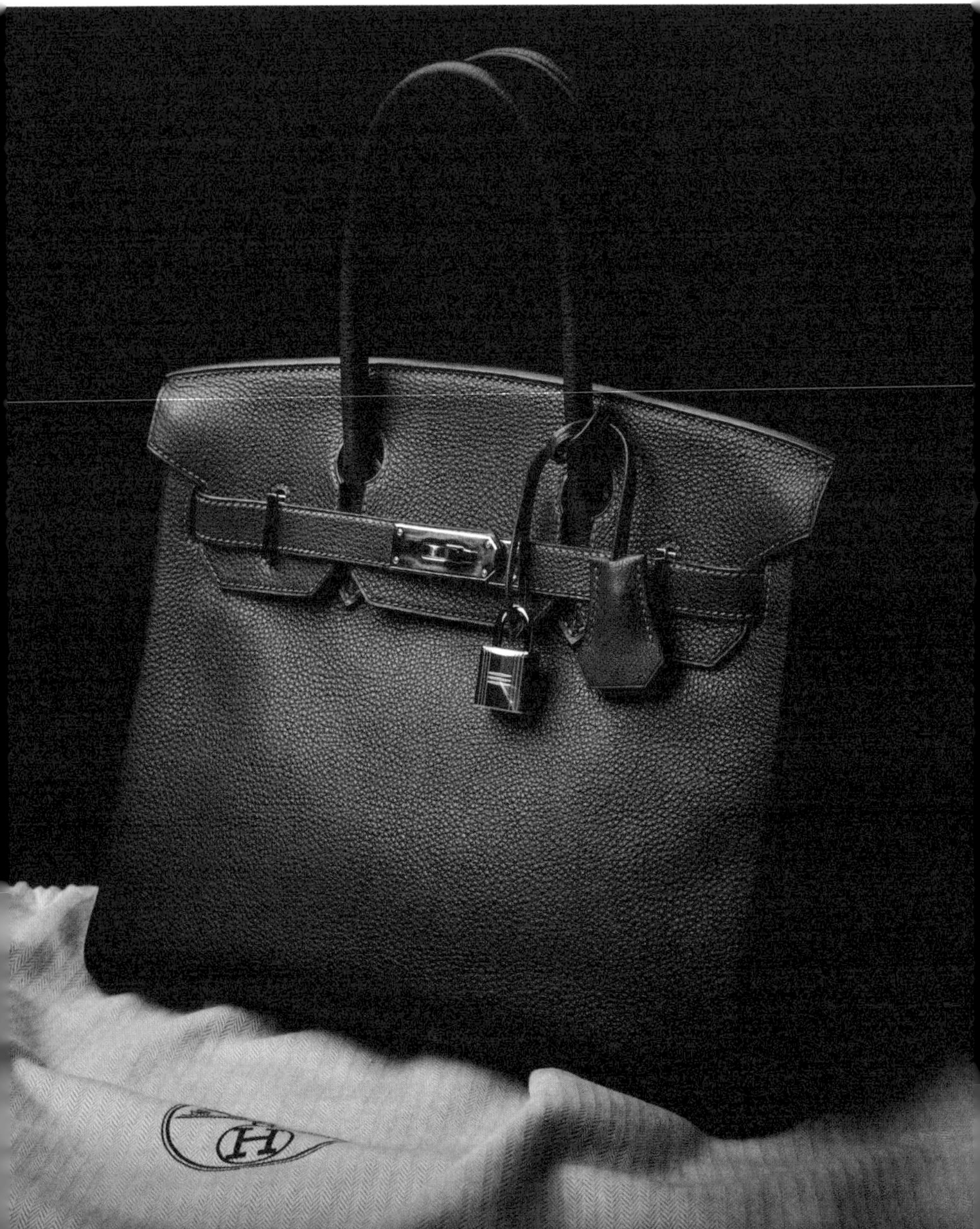

RECENT CLASS ACTION LAWSUIT *Against* HERMÈS

In 2024, there was a class action lawsuit filed against Hermès. The suit alleges that only certain customers with a history of buying things at Hermès are being allowed to buy Birkin or Kelly bags. It's basically saying that only the richest of the rich are given the opportunity to buy the famed handbags, and only if they have purchased other things at the store. The finger is being pointed at the sales associates who work at Hermès, who, it is claimed, suggest that clients buy jewelry, shoes, watches, or other items in order to be qualified in their eyes to buy a treasured Birkin or Kelly bag. Not cool. Or legal, actually. Whoops.

As an unfair business practice that violates antitrust laws, the lawsuit was filed in California by a bunch of disgruntled customers who just want a fair chance to buy a handbag. It's well known that to buy a Birkin or Kelly bag, there is an extensive waitlist to get on. It's much like the waitlist that other luxury companies use for some of their products, such as the Rolex watch and the Ferrari car. Hermès hasn't spoken publicly in response to the lawsuit yet, so it will be interesting to see what happens when they get to court, whenever that might be.

"QUALITY ISN'T JUST ABOUT MATERIALS, IT'S ALSO ABOUT HUMAN SKILL, CREATIVITY, AND THE TIME IT TAKES TO MAKE SOMETHING SPECIAL."

Jean-Paul Gaultier

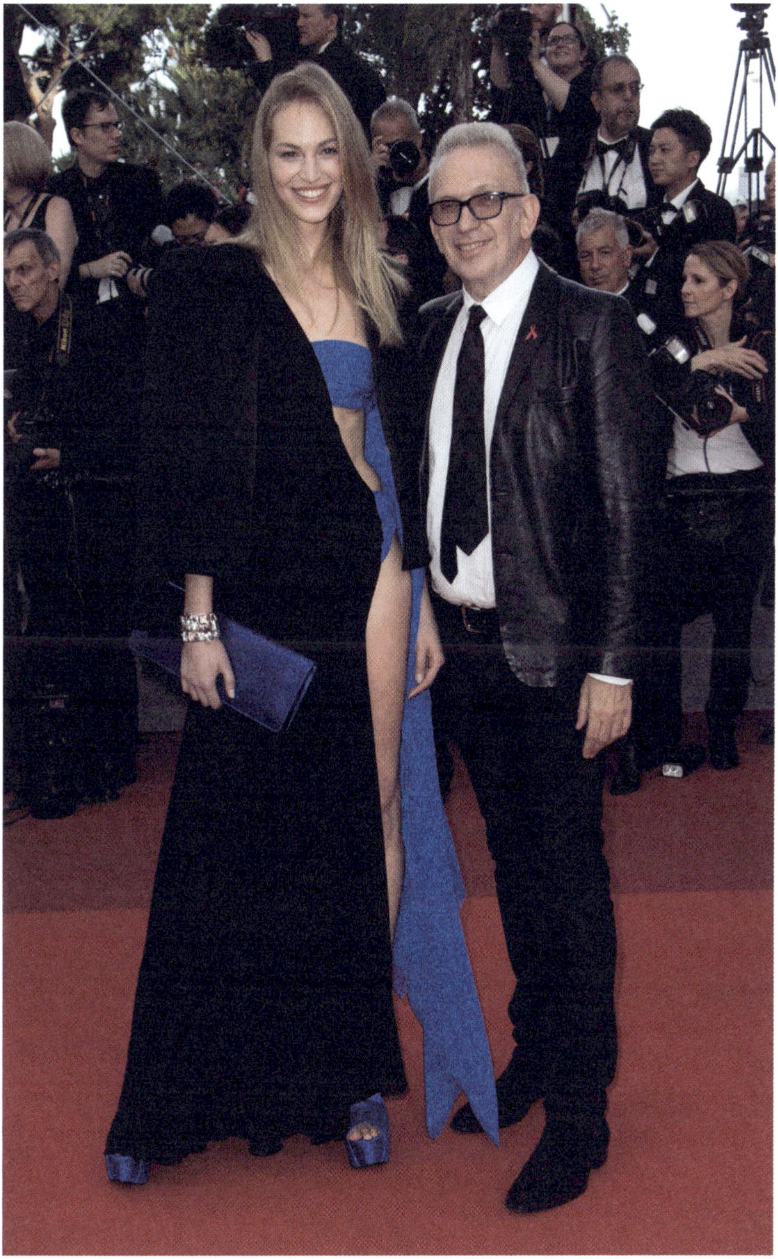

4

The FAMOUS HERMÈS SCARF

Clothing

THERE IS SOMETHING TIMELESS and elegant about a classic Hermès scarf. The original scarf couldn't be more simple: just a large square in silk imported from China. The history of this luxury item dates back to 1937, almost 100 years after the company was created by Thierry Hermès to make equestrian items, when they released the first Hermès scarf. It was meant to be worn in a variety of ways, tied just so. Around the neck, on the head, tossed casually over the shoulders, it was an easy item to wear.

Princess Grace Kelly of Monaco even wore the scarf as a sling when she hurt her arm in 1957. When she was photographed, everyone knew she was wearing a Hermès scarf. Even Elizabeth II, the Queen of England, was a huge fan of the Hermès scarf, adorning her head with it on many occasions when she was out and about. She started wearing these scarves in the 1940s. Jackie Kennedy wore the scarf in much the same way when she was First Lady of the United States. It was a stylish way for a woman to protect her hairstyle from the wind on an outing.

The silk that is used for each Hermès scarf is very strong. Instead of importing it from China, the company now uses its own plants of silkworms in Brazil and Lyon, France. It's an eco-friendly farming co-op that produces extremely high-quality silk for the gorgeous scarves.

EVEN ELIZABE
QUEEN OF ENG

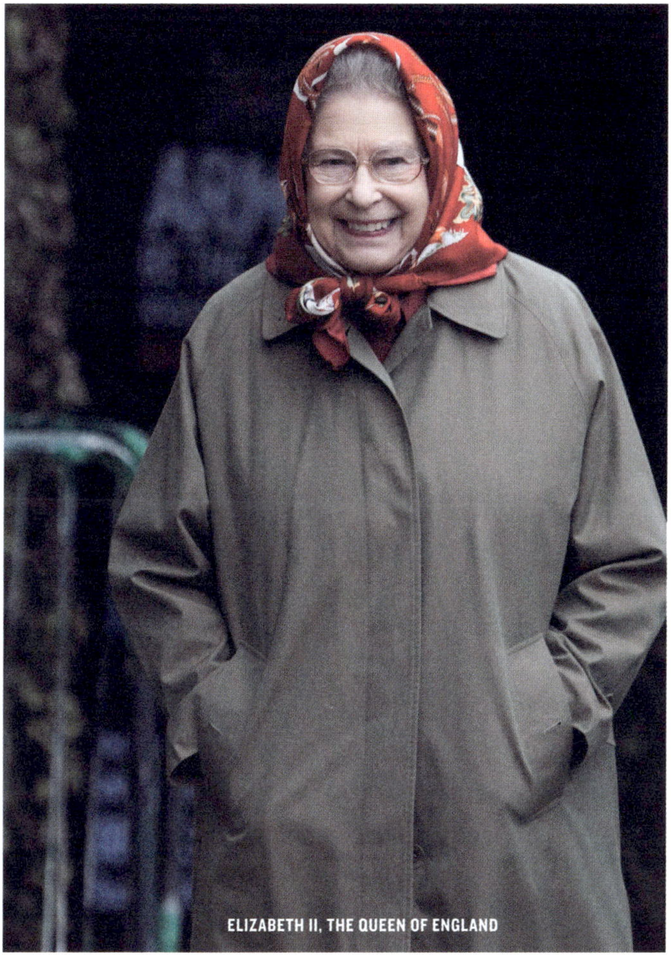

ELIZABETH II, THE QUEEN OF ENGLAND

SHE WAS FIRS
INITED STATE

T

oday, they make a variety of scarves, including a smaller version of the classic called the Twilly. It's a smaller silk accessory that can be tied in a variety of ways. Some people tie it around the neck, or in their hair to secure a ponytail; some even attach it to a handbag as a type of accessory. The Twilly is adorable. Collectible. The most chic item to have.

All of the scarves are made in France and come in a bunch of different styles, colors, patterns, prints, and designs. The Hermès scarf is essentially a wearable piece of art, with thousands of motifs being produced over the years. From start to finish, when Hermès creates a scarf, it takes around 18 months to go from design concept to production. When produced, the scarf is screen printed at a bespoke atelier in France. The printers that they use have to be engraved separately for each new scarf design, and once printed, the stitching on the hem is done by hand.

For each collection every season, they seek out some of the best artists in the world. It's quite an honor to get to make a Hermès scarf design. They release at least 10 new designs per season, and sometimes they reissue popular vintage designs. Here are some of the most famous Hermès designs for their scarves over the years and the year they first came out. Many have been reissued over the years again and again. All of these original scarves are 100 percent silk.

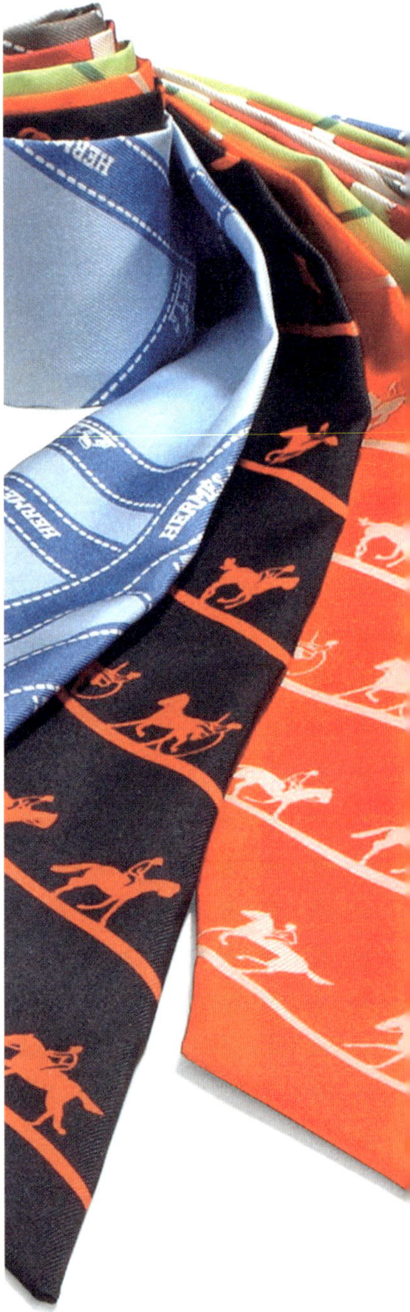

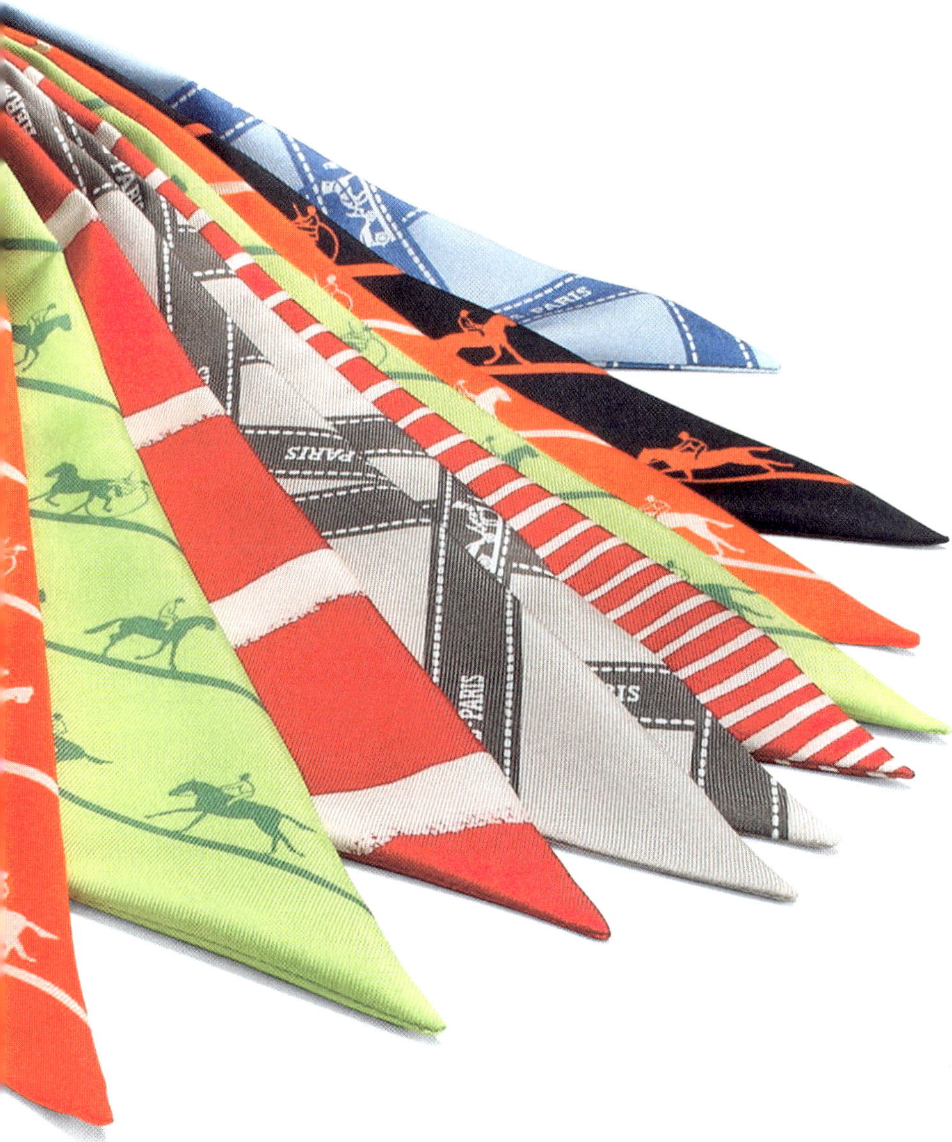
PARIS

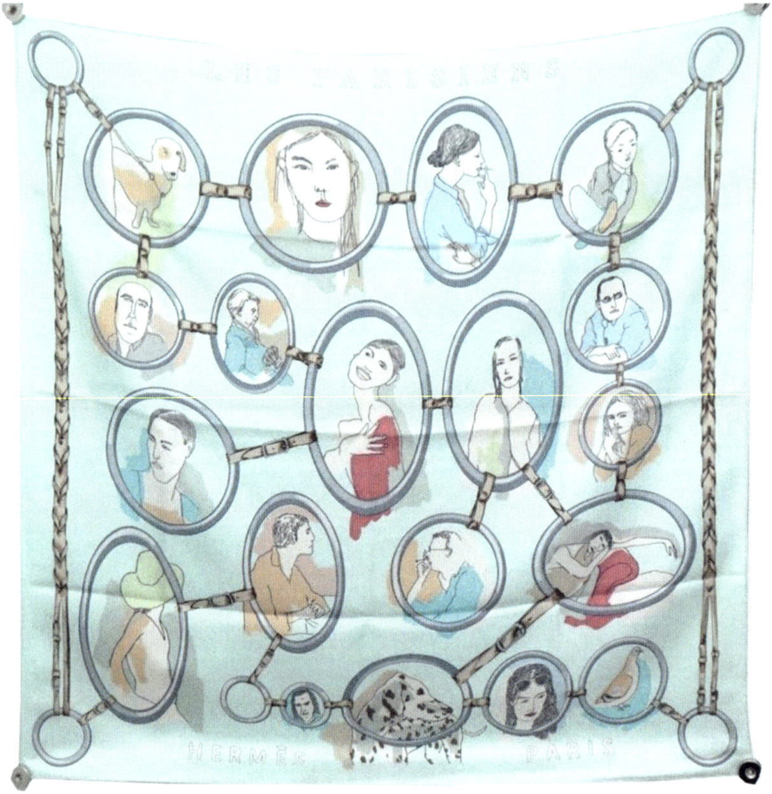

1956

LES PARISIENS

This is an adorably chic scarf that features various French women in different outfits and a couple of dogs. It also showcases iconic Paris landmarks in multicolor with bright hues that make this scarf pop. The edges of Les Parisiens are hand rolled.

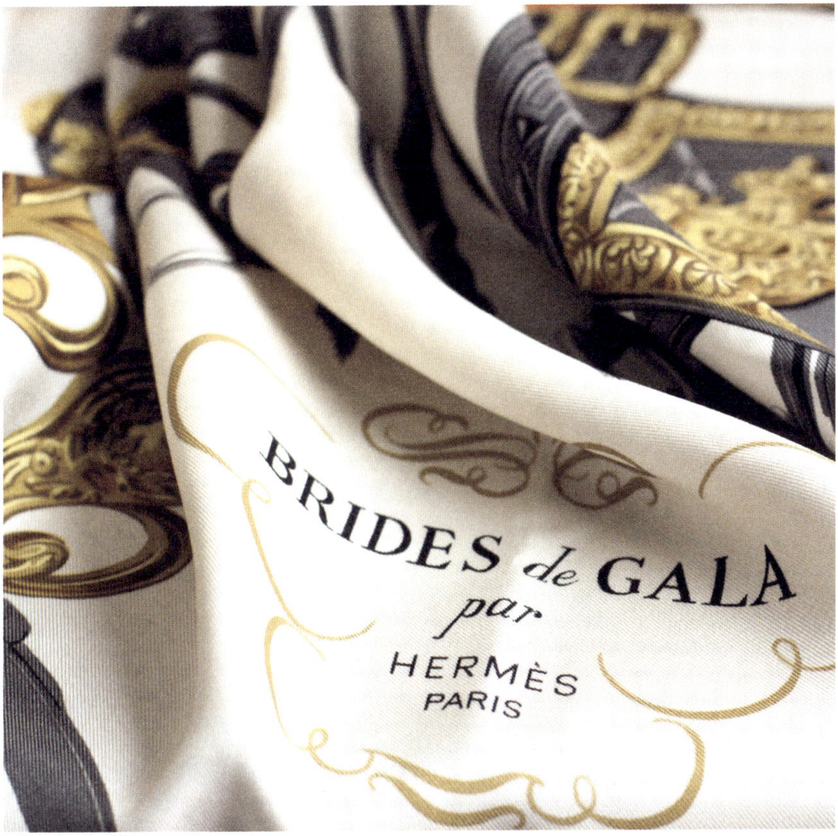

1957

BRIDES DE GALA

One of Hermès' most popular designs, the Brides de Gala scarf has an equestrian theme. It has horse bridle details in black and gold against a cream background with a black frame. The edges are hand rolled on this one as well. Currently, Hermès still sells an original version of this scarf without any design changes, which they call Brides de Gala Forever Scarf 90, for $550.

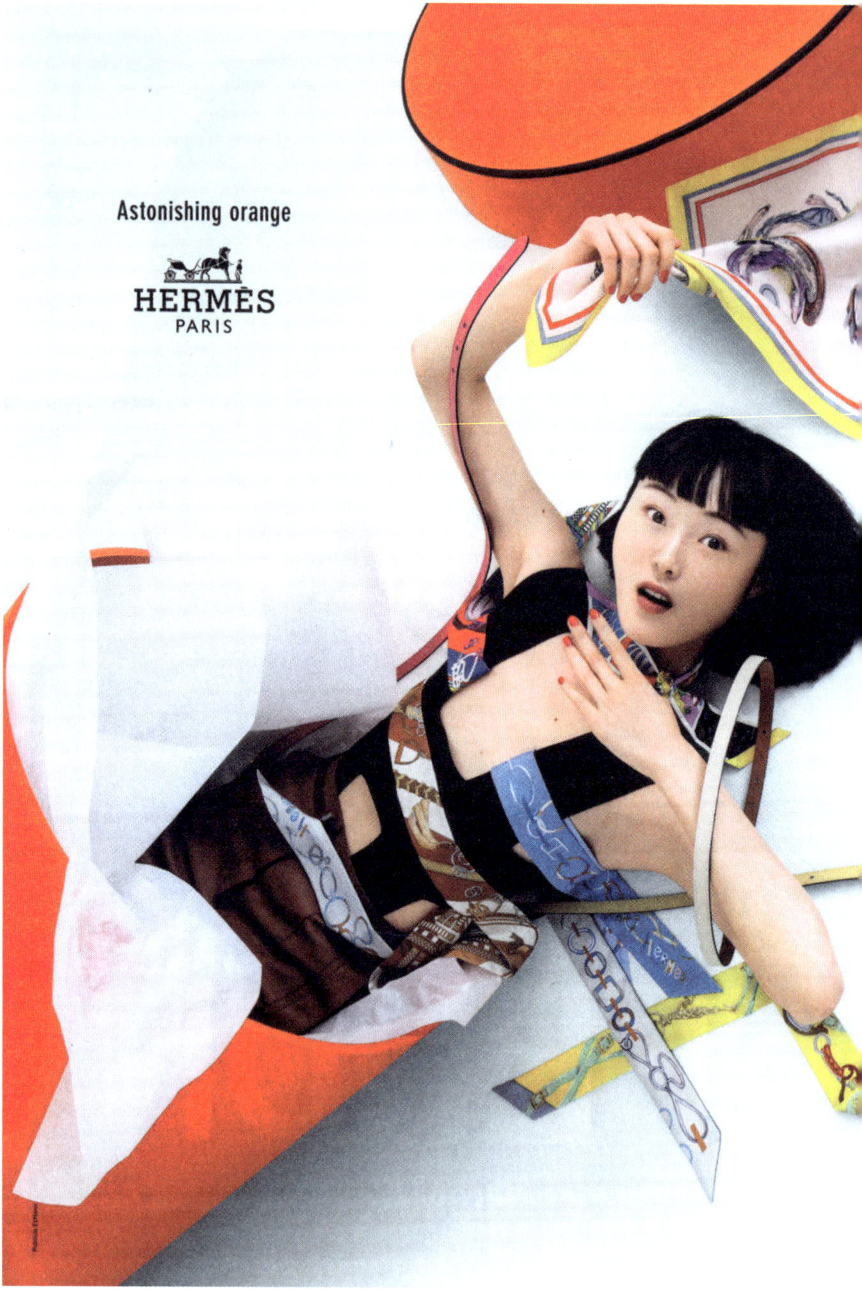
Astonishing orange
HERMÈS
PARIS

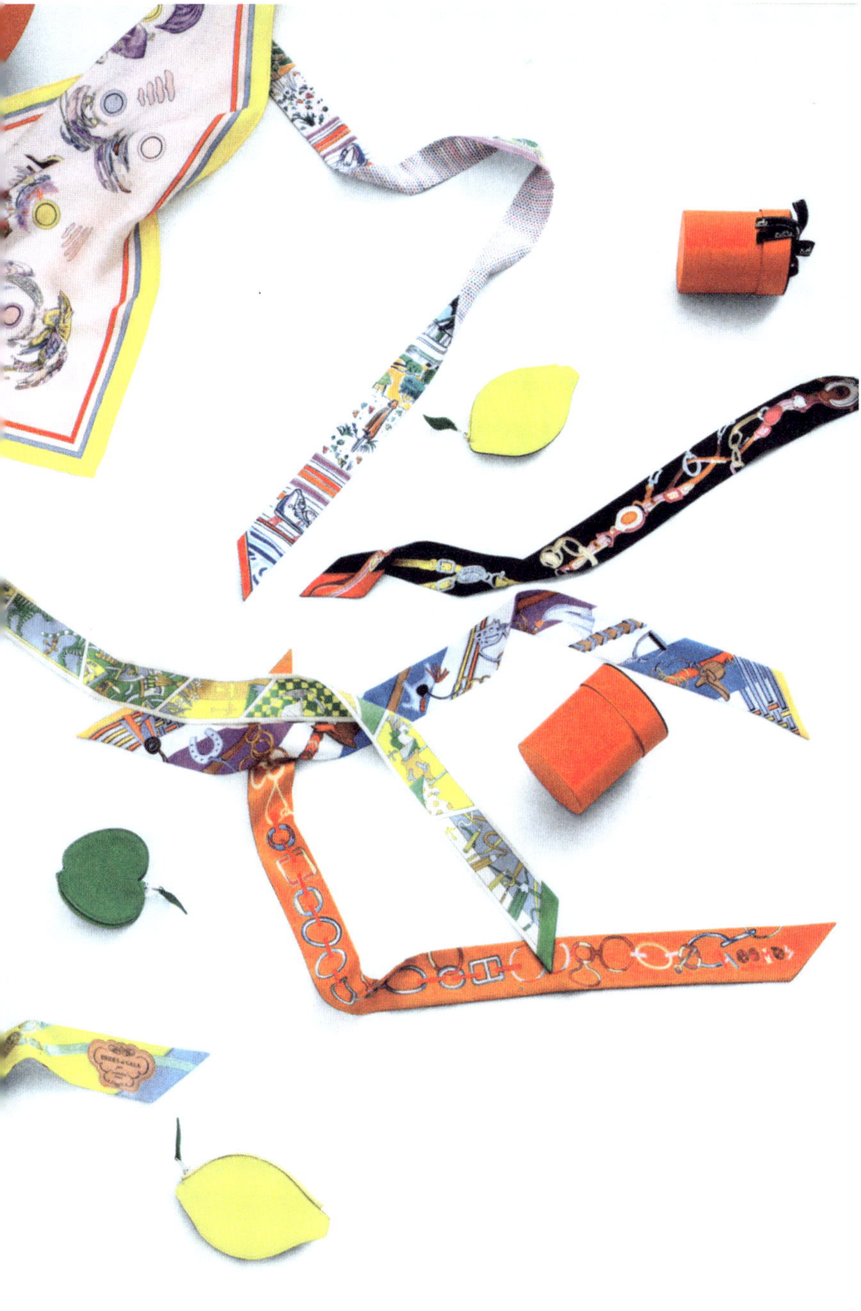

1963

LES CAVALIERS D'OR

This was a limited-edition design with a color palette of gold and black against a backdrop of either red, blue, or cream. Les Cavaliers D'Or also has an equestrian theme; it means "golden rider." It's one of the most sought-after scarves on the resale market.

1963

ASTROLOGIE

Designed in 1963, Astrologie is meant to cater to the lover of the stars. Astrology enthusiasts adore this scarf with its different zodiac signs, stars, and other astrological elements displayed on this glorious work of art. There are lots of vibrant colors on this scarf against a navy blue background, which is obviously meant to represent the night sky. The current version of the scarf is called Astrologie Forever Scarf 90, similar to how they sell the new version of the Brides de Gala.

1965

LES VOITURES A TRANSFORMATION

This fun scarf pictures two different antique cars that can transform into horse-drawn carriages. Car enthusiasts go crazy for this specific scarf. Although it was 100 percent silk when it was originally made in 1965, Hermès now sells an updated version of it, a giant triangle made of a blend of cashmere and silk. But if you want a vintage version, it's fairly easy to find on luxury resale shop websites.

1968

LES POULAINS

Les Poulains is French for "young horse" or "foal." And that's exactly what is on this scarf: a bounty of ponies, and some adult horses, too. This motif is meant to represent the unbridled energy of these magnificent creatures. In the original version, the background is pink and the horses are natural colors, such as brown and tan. Hermès doesn't currently sell an updated version of this scarf.

1970

LES CLES

All over this scarf, there are antique keys. That's why it's named Les Cles, which means "key" in French. Currently, Hermès sells a Les Cles Bandana 55 version of this print predominantly in red, which is silk twill with hand-rolled edges but is smaller than the original (90cm x 90cm). In case you are wondering, there are 47 keys displayed on this classic scarf.

2007

CAVALCADOUR

Another fun choice for horse lovers, the Cavalcadour is one of the most recent favorites. Today, it comes in a Twilly and not the full version. The French word means a rush of animals for this creative scarf. The background of this scarf was white with colorful details, but the new Twilly comes in five different color themes, such as "Marine, Gold, and Gris."

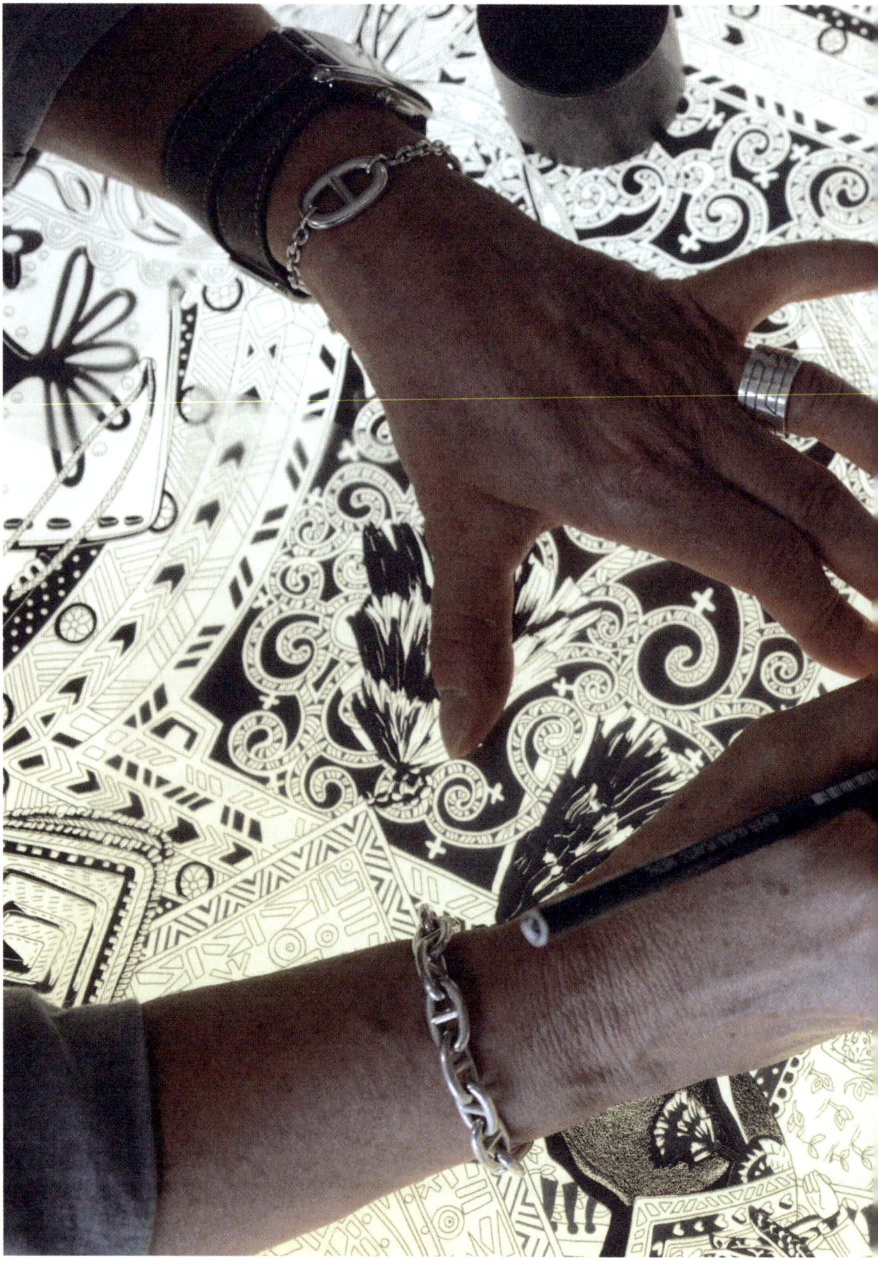

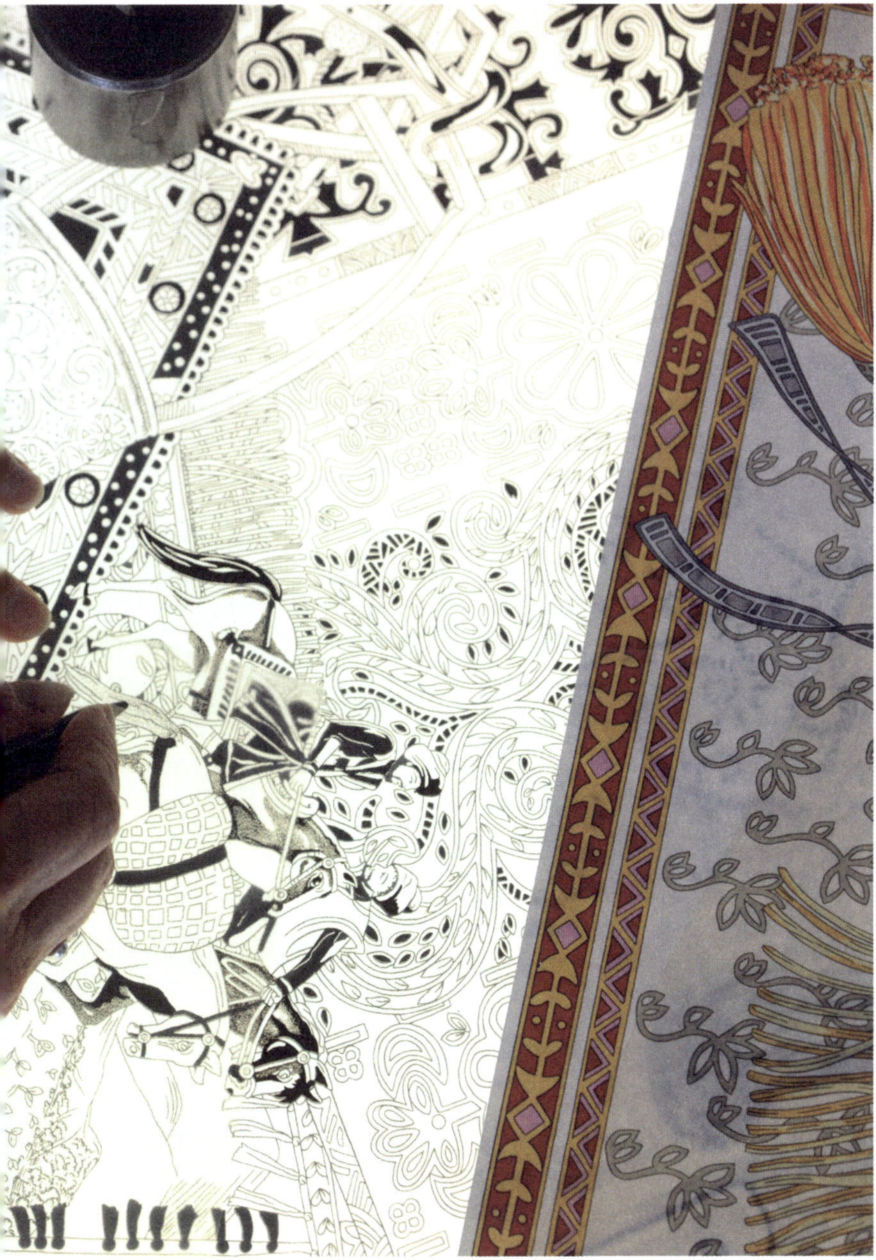

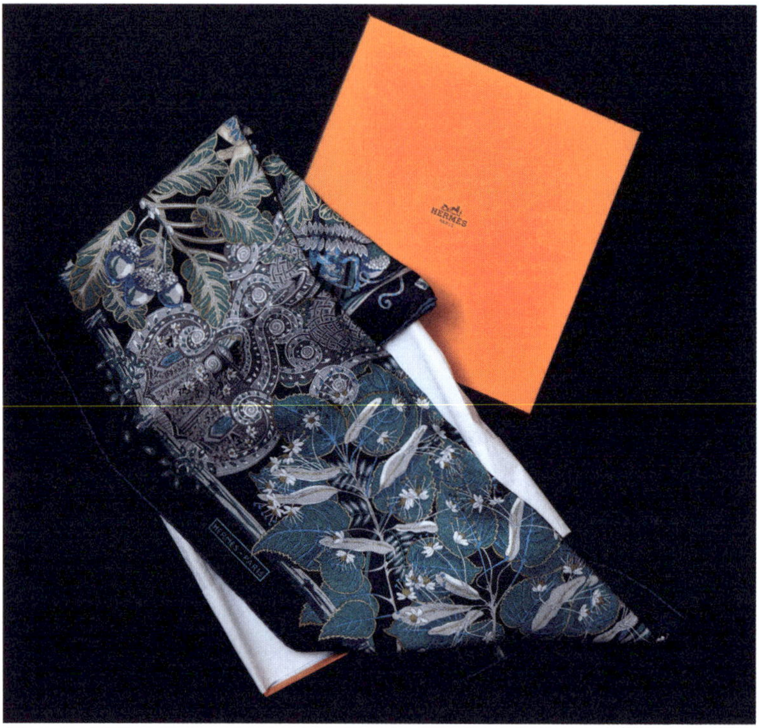

2011

MYTHES *ET* MÉTAMOR-PHOSES

Designed with meticulous attention to detail, this scarf is a work of art that weaves together ancient tales and contemporary elegance. Each motif on the scarf tells a story, from the mythical creatures of ancient Greece to the transformative power of nature. Whether it's the graceful dance of a nymph, the majestic flight of Pegasus, or the mysterious allure of Medusa, every element is rendered with exquisite precision and craftsmanship.

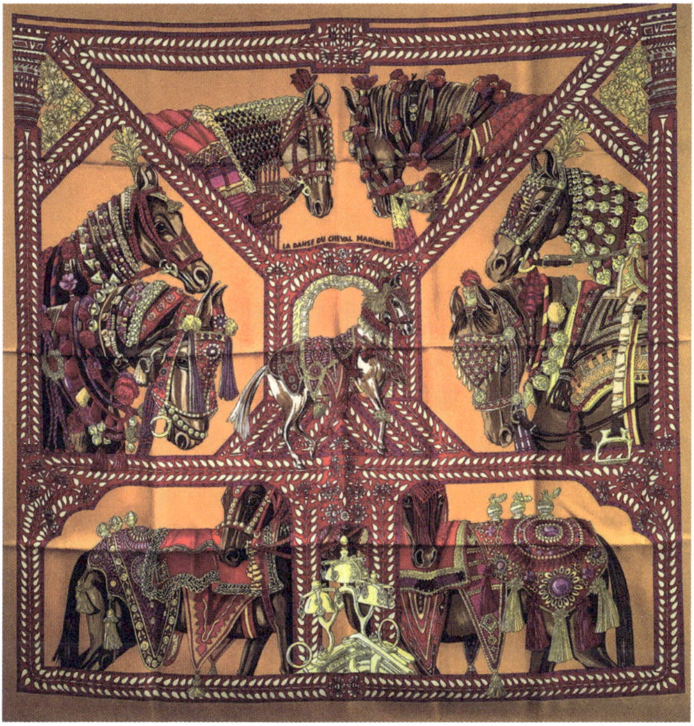

2014

LA DANSE *DU* CHEVAL MARWARI

A festive scarf that features a traditional Indian dance with horses that are called Marwari. This is a multicolored scarf that is mostly red, purple, and pink. It's gorgeous with beautiful detailing in designs where the horses are decked out in all kinds of finery. There isn't a version of this scarf sold today, but it's easy enough to find on different luxury resale sites.

"HERMES IS THE PINNACLE OF *LUXURY*. THEIR PRODUCTS ARE *ICONIC* AND ALWAYS MAKE A *STATEMENT*."

Kim Kardashian

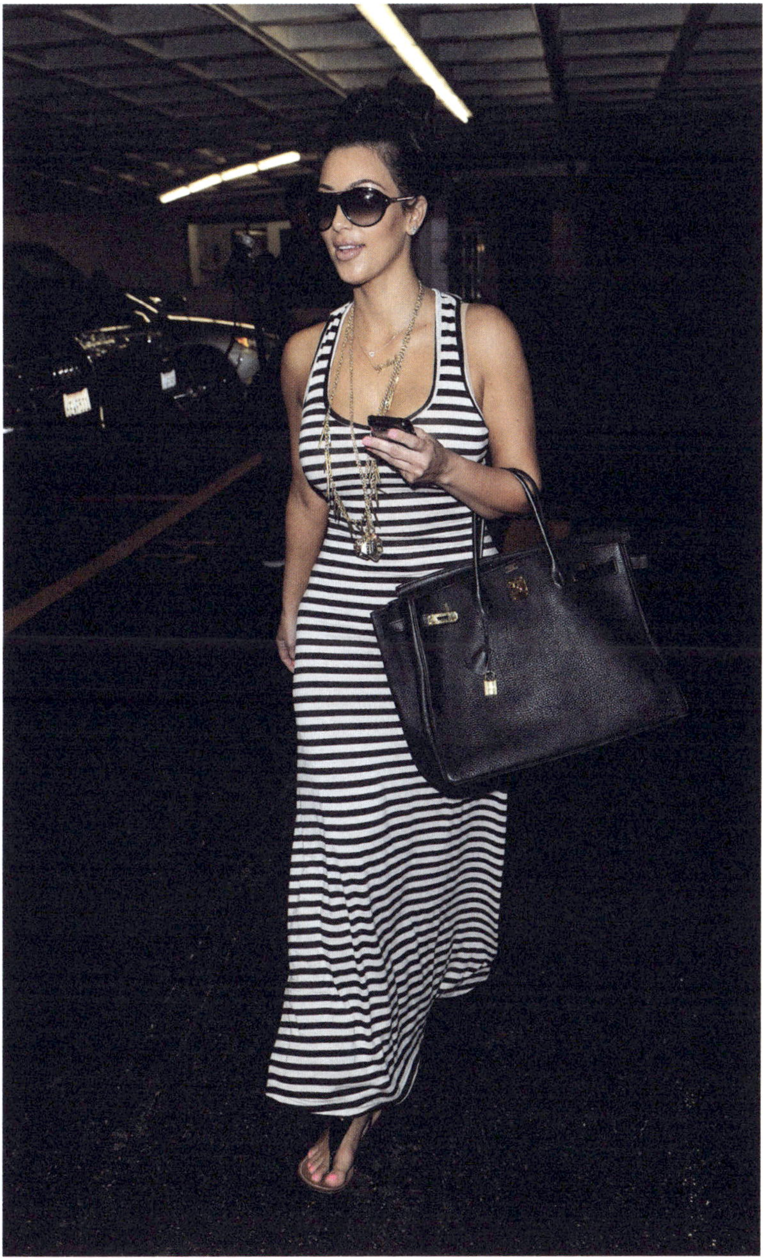

5

WATCHES, JEWELRY, GIFTS, *and* HOME

Accessories & Home

HERMÈS MAKES A VARIETY OF WATCHES, jewelry, gifts, and lifestyle accessories for the home that make the most lovely presents. When you give someone Hermès, you are giving them a piece of living history, unparalleled craftsmanship, and the utmost elegance from one of the most recognized luxury brands in the world. Here are some of the most loved and interesting items that Hermès sells today.

WATCHES

Hermès timepieces and watches are a huge status symbol. Although they started making watches for the public in 1928, the very first Hermès watch was created in 1912 for the great-granddaughter of the founder of the brand, Thierry Hermès. But when they started making them for the public, they partnered with Swiss watchmaker Movado.

Today, they have all kinds of modern designs that still pay homage to the classics they created so long ago. There is even a partnership with Apple for the Hermès Apple Watch, which has different sporty color options, an interlocking "H" motif, and a band that is inspired by a golfing glove that Hermès created in the 1930s. If you want a very classy smartwatch, the Hermès Apple Watch is the way to go. Otherwise, here are a few of the classics they offer today in women's timepieces.

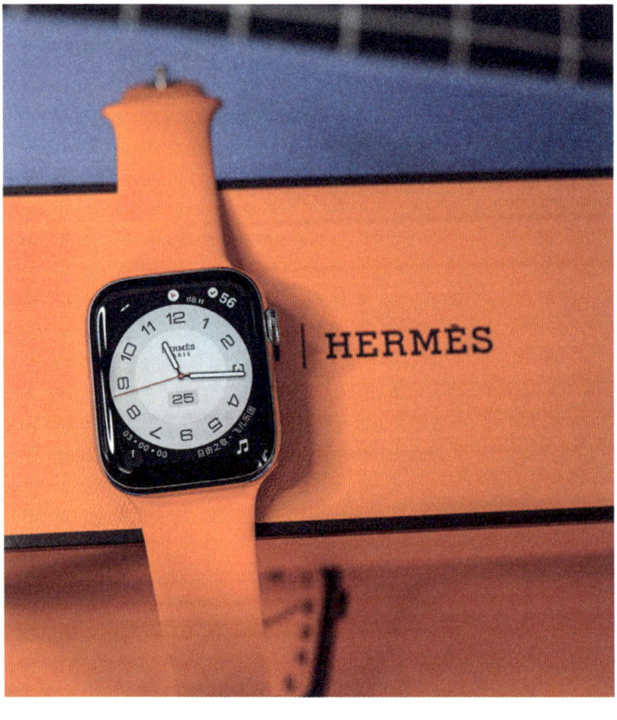

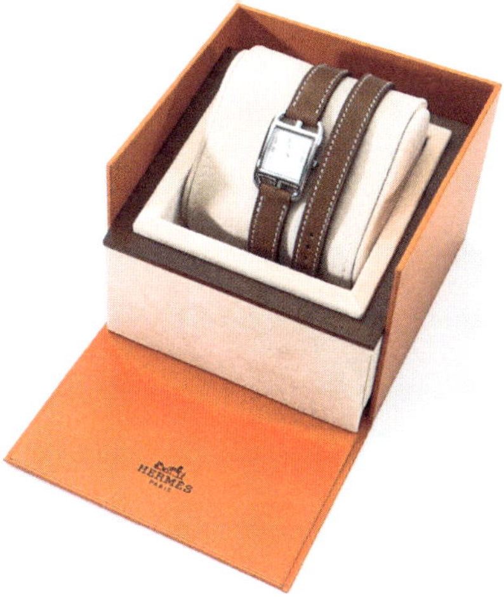

CAPE COD

The Cape Cod is a cool watch to have. It's a small square-shaped face in stainless steel that comes in a small or large size with a ton of different options to choose from. The classic one to get has a wrap-around leather strap in Barenia calfskin. You can change out the straps for variety as well. If you want to truly splurge, get the one that has a face surrounded by diamonds set in rose gold with a sapphire blue strap. It's absolutely stunning.

KELLY

You may think of the famous Hermès Kelly bag, but they also make it in a watch. They call it the Kelly due to the watch face being the same lock that is on the Kelly bag. They make three styles of this watch in a mini size made from steel. The base watch doesn't have any diamonds, but the other two do. The most expensive model has diamonds around the face of the watch but also set in the bracelet strap. The padlock watch face is detachable, so technically, you could take it off and wear it on a necklace.

HERMÈS CUT

This watch is probably the most traditional design of the ones they offer. It's a round face in 10 different styles. You can have it with diamonds, stainless steel, or mixed metals. There are different band styles available that you can switch out as well. This is a large-faced watch that is water resistant up to 100 meters. It's the ideal everyday watch that is easy to wear and goes with everything.

JEWELRY

Hermès makes a variety of fashion jewelry, gold, and silver pieces. They are famous for their enamel bracelets in all different sizes, materials, and patterns. Think of it like a piece of wearable art for your wrist, much like the classic Hermès scarf. They come out with different styles of enamel bracelets all the time. Here are a few classic Hermès jewelry pieces that are worth adding to your collection.

KELLY CLOCHETTE RING

This is an adorable ring that pays tribute to the Kelly bag, of course. It's a white gold and diamond charm ring that has a "clochette" charm, which, on the Kelly bag, holds the key. There is also a key charm on the ring. Diamonds wrap around the band. This would be the perfect graduation gift for a first luxury jewelry piece.

CHAINE D'ANCRE CHAOS EARRINGS

Dangly rose gold earrings set with diamonds, the Chaine d'ancre motif is a famous Hermès style that has been used in countless collections. It was inspired in 1937 by the anchor chains that held the ships in place on the Normandy coast of France. These are subtle enough and the right size for everyday wear.

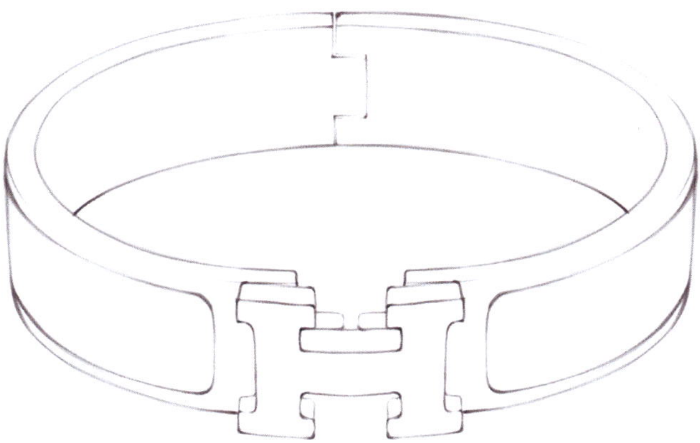

GIFTS AND HOME

Opening up a classic Hermès box for any occasion, such as a birthday, a holiday, a wedding, or a baby shower, is a grand event. Just the sight of that famed orange and brown box is enough to put a smile on anyone's face. Here are a few of the gifts that Hermès offers today.

CANOPÉE LE SON DU H VASE

The ideal wedding present, this vase is porcelain with a cork base in white and blue. H lettering is all over it, and it would look stunning on a hallway entrance table in a Park Avenue apartment in New York City. Okay, no matter where you live, this is a gorgeously large vase to display a weekly arrival of flowers.

MONSIEUR B TOTE BAG

This fun tote bag is part of the Petit h collection, which is a gift line inspired by artisan creation. The Monsieur B Tote Bag is a two-toned bag that comes in canvas and calfskin. The fun part about ordering this bag is that the color is going to be a surprise. It's an ideal bag to carry around everyday essentials or take to the grocery store for a reusable bag when you only need to grab a few things.

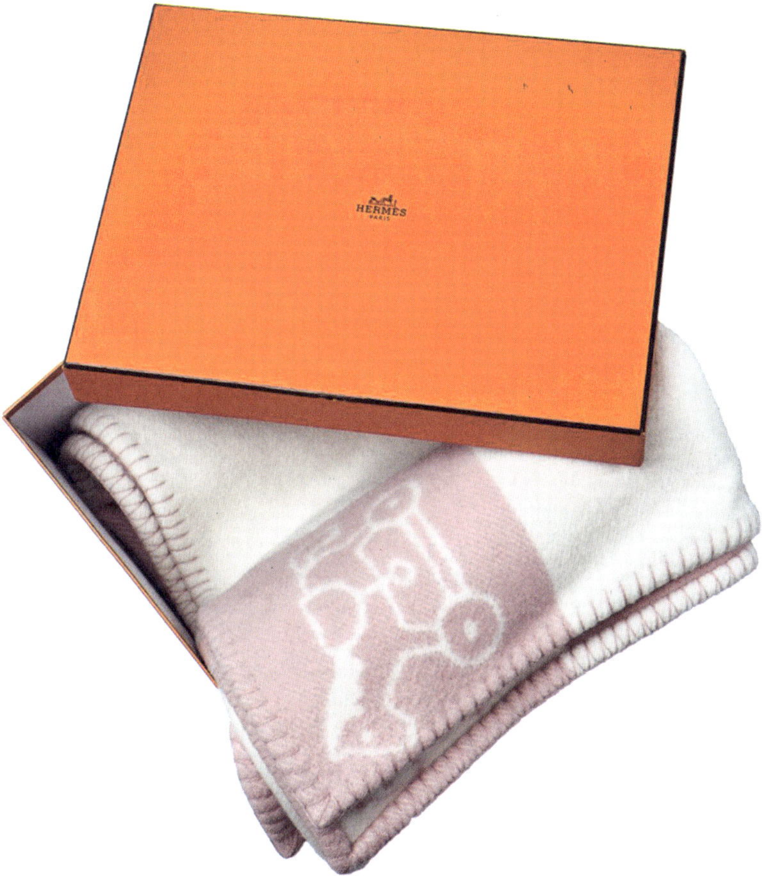

AVALON BABY BLANKET

The Hermès Avalon Baby Blanket is a gorgeous gift for parents about to have a new bundle of joy. It's wool and cashmere with "H" lettering all over it. The color choices are cream with tan, blue, and pink. Soft and snuggly, this will become your baby's favorite blanket as they grow.

"HERMÈS EMBODIES THE *ESSENCE OF LUXURY AND STYLE*. ITS PIECES ARE TIMELESS CLASSICS THAT ADD A TOUCH OF *SOPHISTICATION* TO ANY WARDROBE"

Heidi Klum

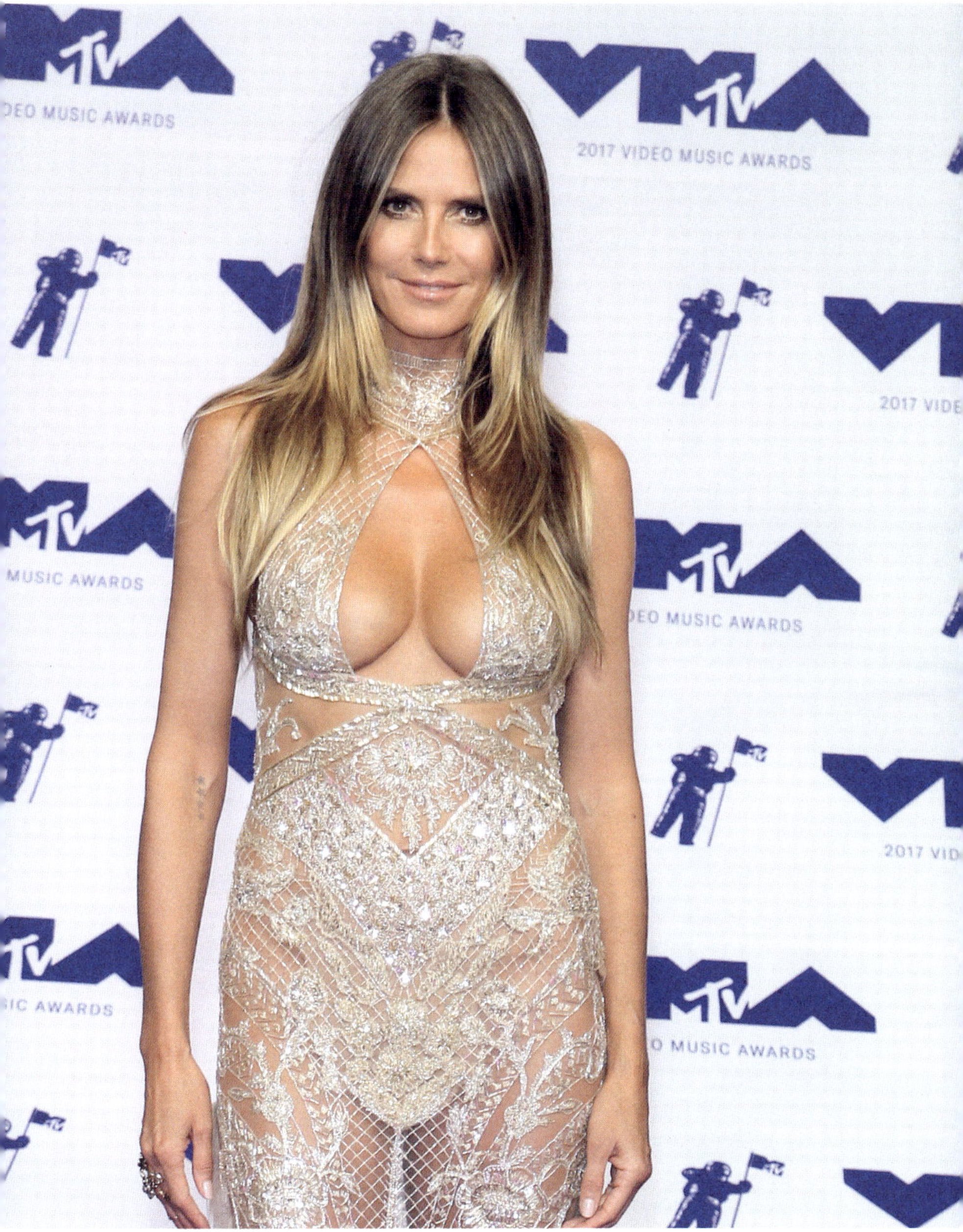
MTV
2017 VIDEO MUSIC AWARDS

6

THE BIRKIN, THE KELLY BAG, *and More*

Handbags

THE FIRST LEATHER HANDBAGS were introduced by Hermès in 1922. Of course, when people think of handbags and the luxury maker, the Birkin and the Kelly bag are the most recognizable. So where did these two fabulous handbags come from? Let's look at the history of these iconic bags and a few more that Hermès makes that you might not know about.

THE BIRKIN BAG

The story of the Birkin bag doesn't begin in a design studio or atelier but rather on an airplane, of all places, in 1983. The legend has it that Jane Birkin, a popular model and actress, was boarding a plane carrying a large basket for her carry-on items. Jane was known as a fashion icon through the 60s and 70s, especially when she was in a relationship with Serge Gainsbourg, who was a writer and director. They were both pillars of the French pop culture scene.

That evening, when Jane boarded an airplane, she ran into Jean-Louis Dumas on a late-night flight to London from Paris. He was the CEO of Hermès at the time and also the great-grandson of the founder of the company, Thierry Hermès. When Jean-Louis saw Jane struggling with her giant basket as a handbag trying to cram it into the overhead, he laughed with her that she needed a better handbag with pockets. Each obviously knew who the other was, and she told him that if Hermès made the perfect handbag for her that would carry all the items that she needed as a busy mom, she would use it instead of her basket.

So, together on the plane, Jean-Louis with Jane's input sketched up the beginning of the Birkin bag. A year later, the Birkin was launched. Of course, they sent Jane the first bag. It was a 40cm size, although today it comes in four different sizes: 25cm, 30cm, 35cm, and 40cm. When it came out back then, it cost around $2,000. Today, the prices vary widely depending on the material and edition the Birkin comes in. You can expect to find a basic one for around $10,000 to $35,000. Some specialty models can go as high as $2 million.

Jane herself sold that original Birkin in 2011 for charity. It went for $162,000. If you think she had loads and loads of Birkin bags in her closet, you'd be mistaken. She was known to only keep one Birkin bag at a time, other than the first one she was given that she had since 1984.

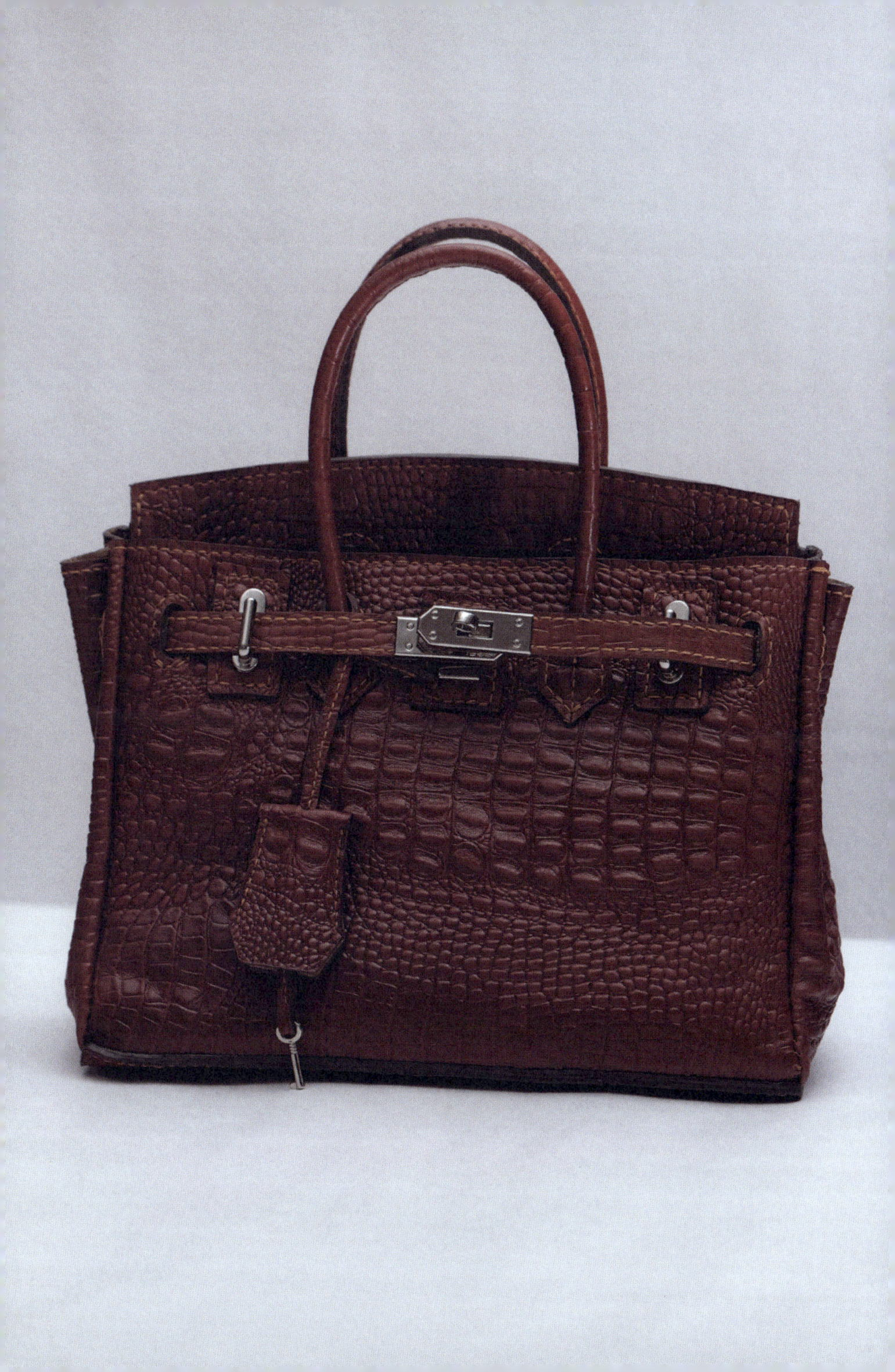

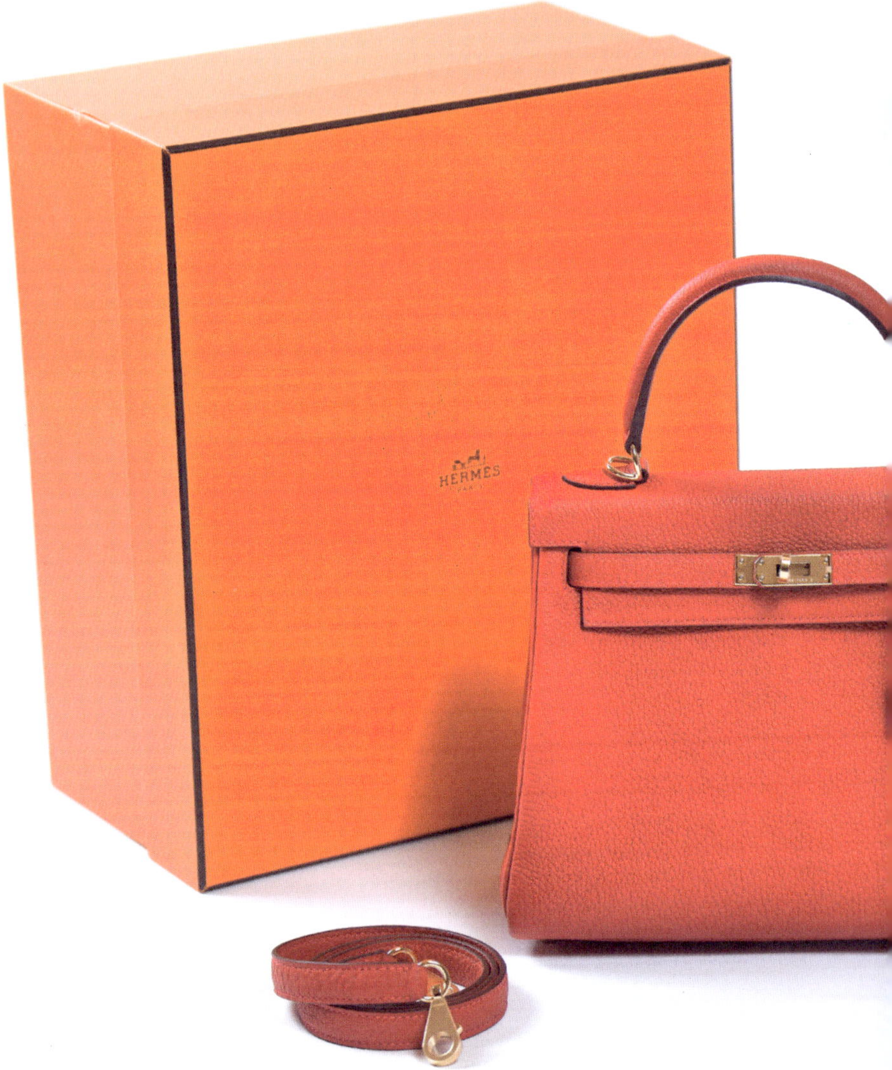
HERMÈS

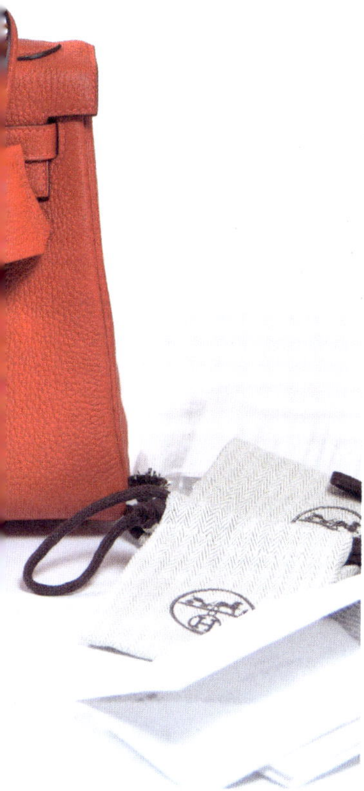

Jane recently passed away in 2023 at the age of 76. Even though she was very famous as a model and actress, she did joke that she would only be remembered for the Hermès Birkin handbag, saying "Bless me when I'm dead, people will possibly only talk about the bag." Incidentally, even though there is a constant waitlist for the Birkin bag at Hermès stores, sales on resale websites went through the roof when Jane died. Demand for the Kelly bag and the Birkin is usually about a 50/50 split, but when Jane passed, demand for the Birkin rose to around 70 percent.

So what does a classic Hermès Birkin look like? The Hermès website describes it as "a supple and spacious rectangular holdall with a burnished flap and saddle stitching." The leather is vegetable-tanned natural cowhide in the basic model, but it can come in exotic materials such as ostrich, crocodile, alligator, and lizard.

The special edition Birkins are truly works of art. One of the best ones they offer right now is the Birkin Faubourg Tropical. It's a jungle pattern embroidered on the front of the bag designed by artists Octave Marsal and Theo de Gueltzal. The leather at the top flap and handle is white. This is a gorgeous bag that you can picture some lucky person carrying around on the Amalfi Coast of southern Italy.

If you are privileged enough to snag yourself a Birkin bag, either from the store's long waitlist or through a verified resale site, it's something that you'll never want to let go. The Birkin is one of the most famous bags in fashion history. Of course, it's not the only bag that Hermès makes: The Kelly is another biggie for the brand.

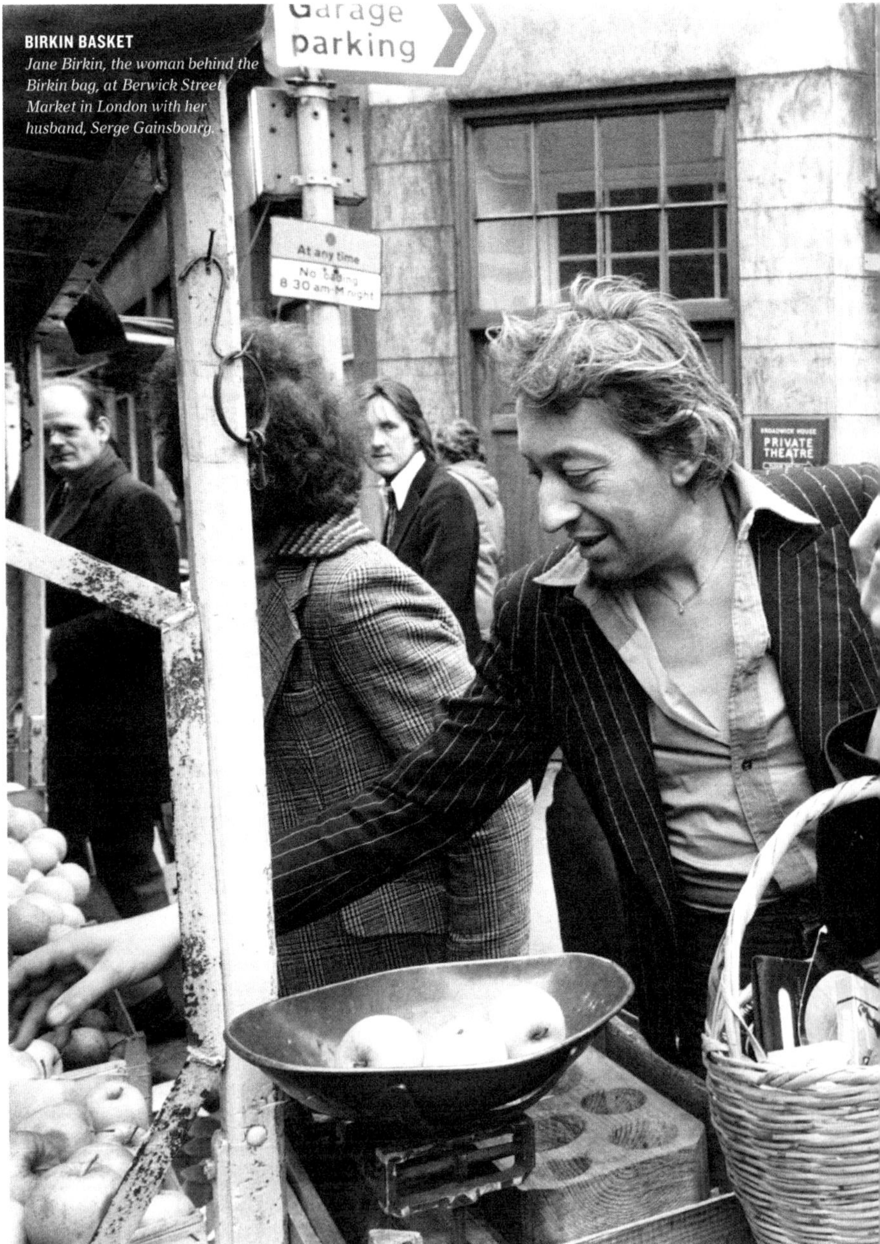

BIRKIN BASKET

Jane Birkin, the woman behind the Birkin bag, at Berwick Street Market in London with her husband, Serge Gainsbourg.

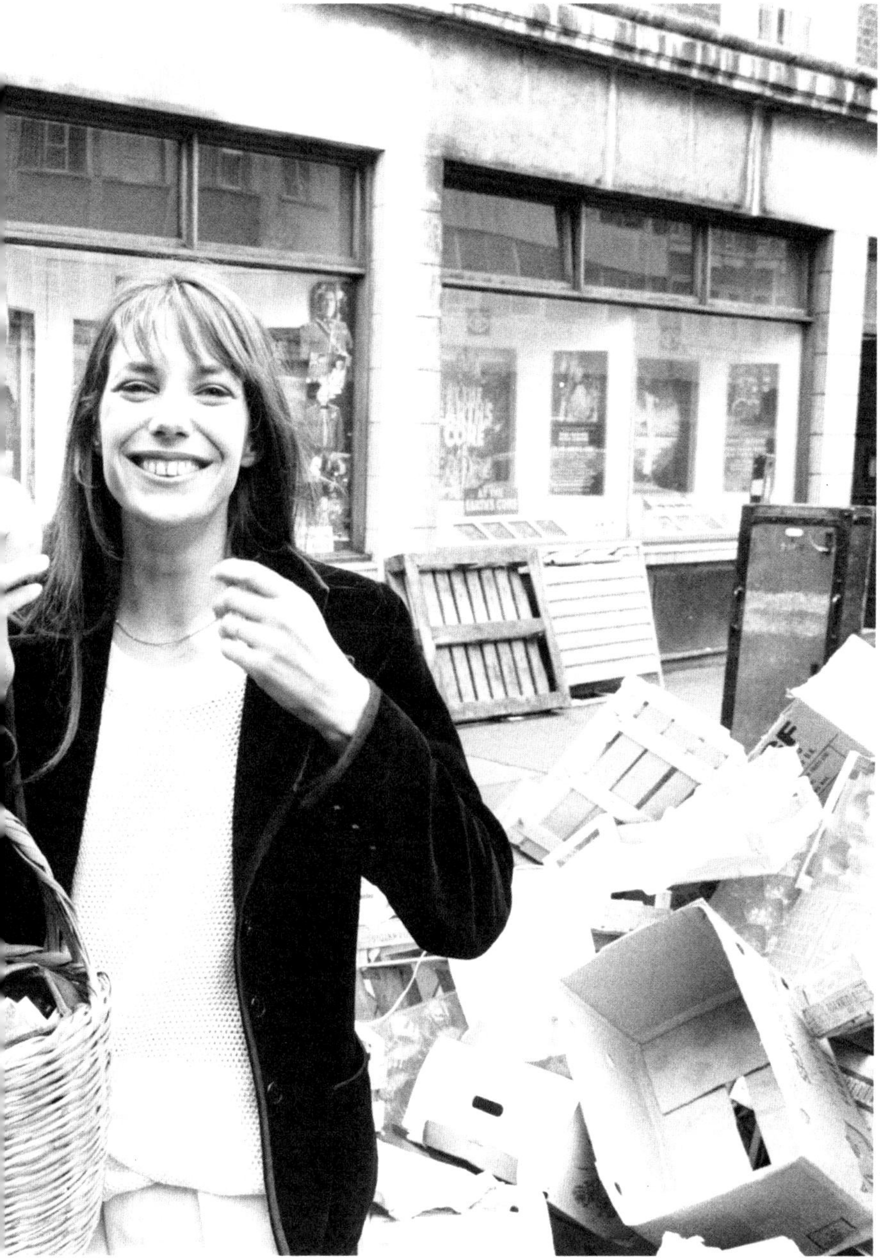

THE KELLY BAG

The origins of the Kelly bag can be seen in the very first saddle bag that Hermès made in 1892. It was called the Haut à courroies. In 1928, Robert Dumas made a smaller version of the bag that he called the Sac à dépêches, which meant "dispatch bag." Women immediately liked it because of its smaller trapezoid shape that was easy to carry. Still, it didn't skyrocket to fame until 1955.

Famous actress Grace Kelly carried the bag in a movie she was in: "To Catch a Thief." She starred alongside Cary Grant in this Alfred Hitchcock classic. The Sac à dépêches was part of her wardrobe as a woman in high society in the movie. When she was done filming the movie, the story goes that she loved the Hermès bag so much that she kept it. That was a stroke of luck for the luxury brand.

Just two years later, Grace married Prince Rainier II of Monaco in a fairytale wedding where she was crowned Princess Grace. Shortly thereafter, she became pregnant and was photographed with the Hermès bag over her stomach. This photo became very famous and was even featured on the cover of Life Magazine, an iconic publication that everyone read. Women all over the world wanted the bag Princess Grace was seen carrying. In today's terms, imagine if Taylor Swift, Beyonce, or even Megan Markle is photographed carrying something fashionable: Demand for it goes through the roof.

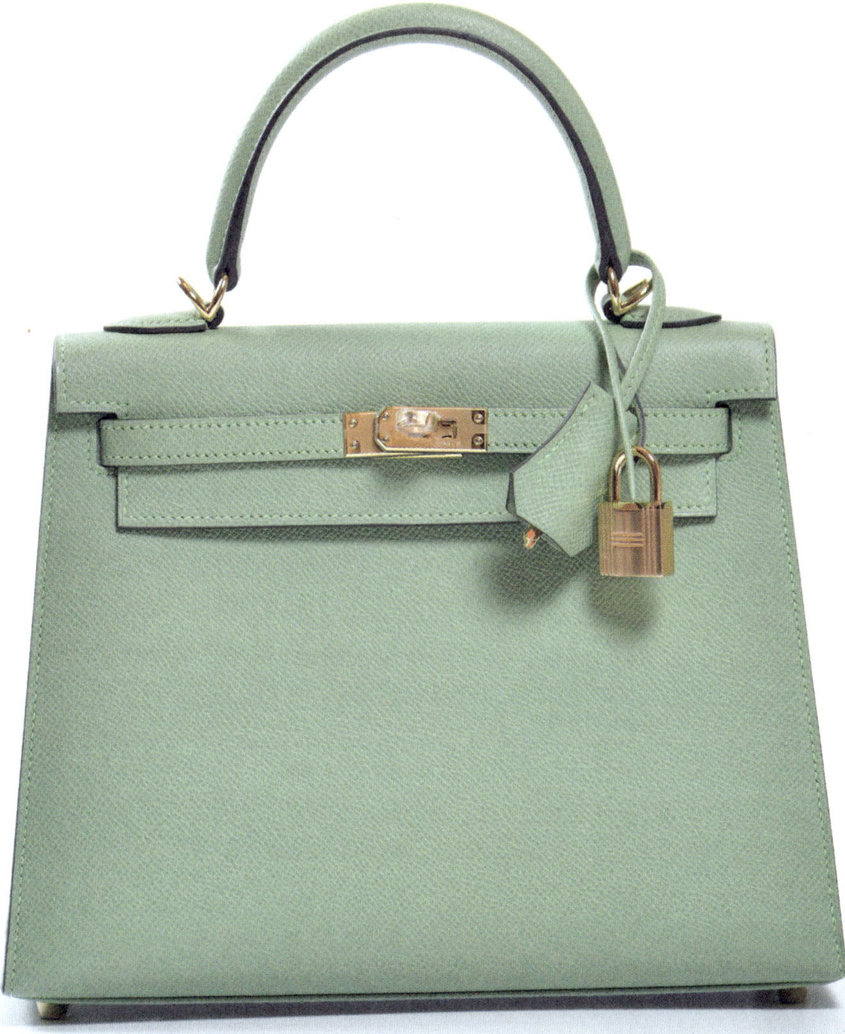

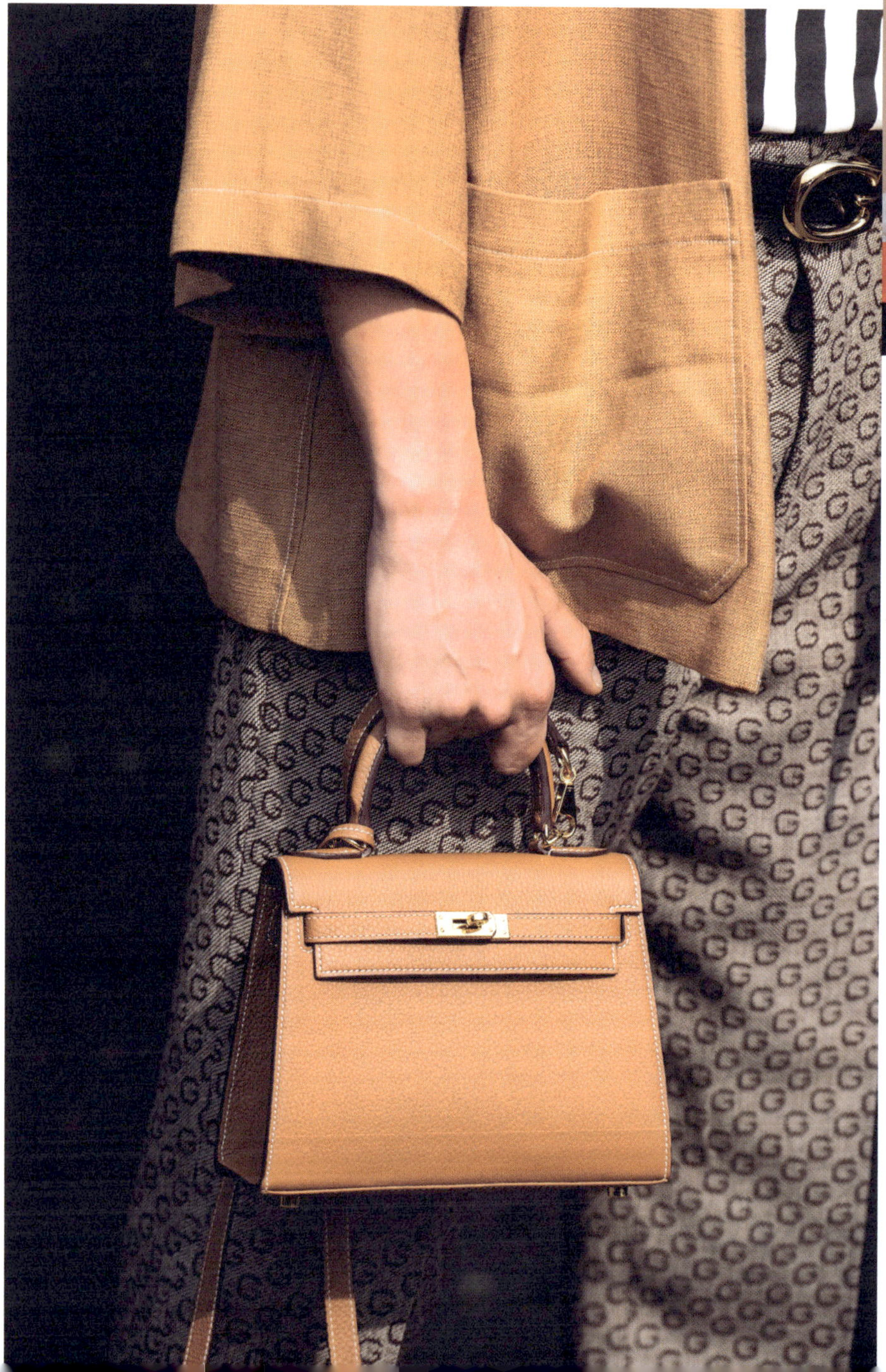

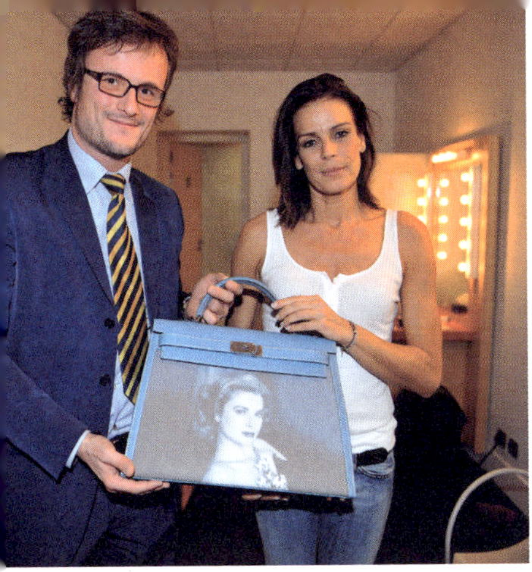

HONORING GRACE

Princess Stephanie poses with a specially designed Hermès 'Kelly' bag, adorned with a portrait of the late Princess Grace.

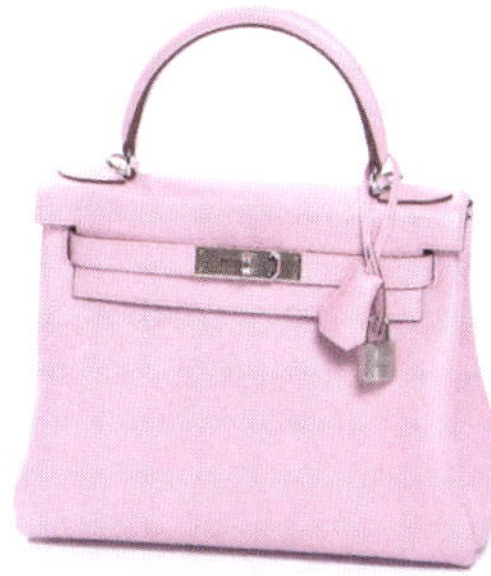

Even though that all happened with Princess Grace in the 50s, Hermès didn't officially change the name of the Sac à dépêches to the Kelly bag until 1977. The Kelly bag comes in eight different sizes from 15cm to 50cm. The range of materials is the same as the Birkin, with many special and limited editions being released over the years.

The style of the Kelly bag is a trapezoid, top-handle bag. It has a detachable shoulder strap with a touret clasp and padlock. From mini to maxi sizes, it's the ideal bag for everyday carry to hold all your essentials. The two main styles are the Sellier and the Retourne: The first is more structured, and the second is a more relaxed style with softer seams to carry more. There have been many limited editions over the years, such as the Kelly Doll bag, which was introduced in 2000 and made for five years. These pint-sized buddy bags were huge hits, only a little bigger than a large smartphone, and came in eight different colors. The Kelly Doll bags looked like they had little faces and feet on them. So cute!

If you want one today, they are only available if you specially order a custom-designed bag with a logo horseshoe stamp on the front. Very exclusive and expensive and practically impossible to come by without knowing someone at Hermès.

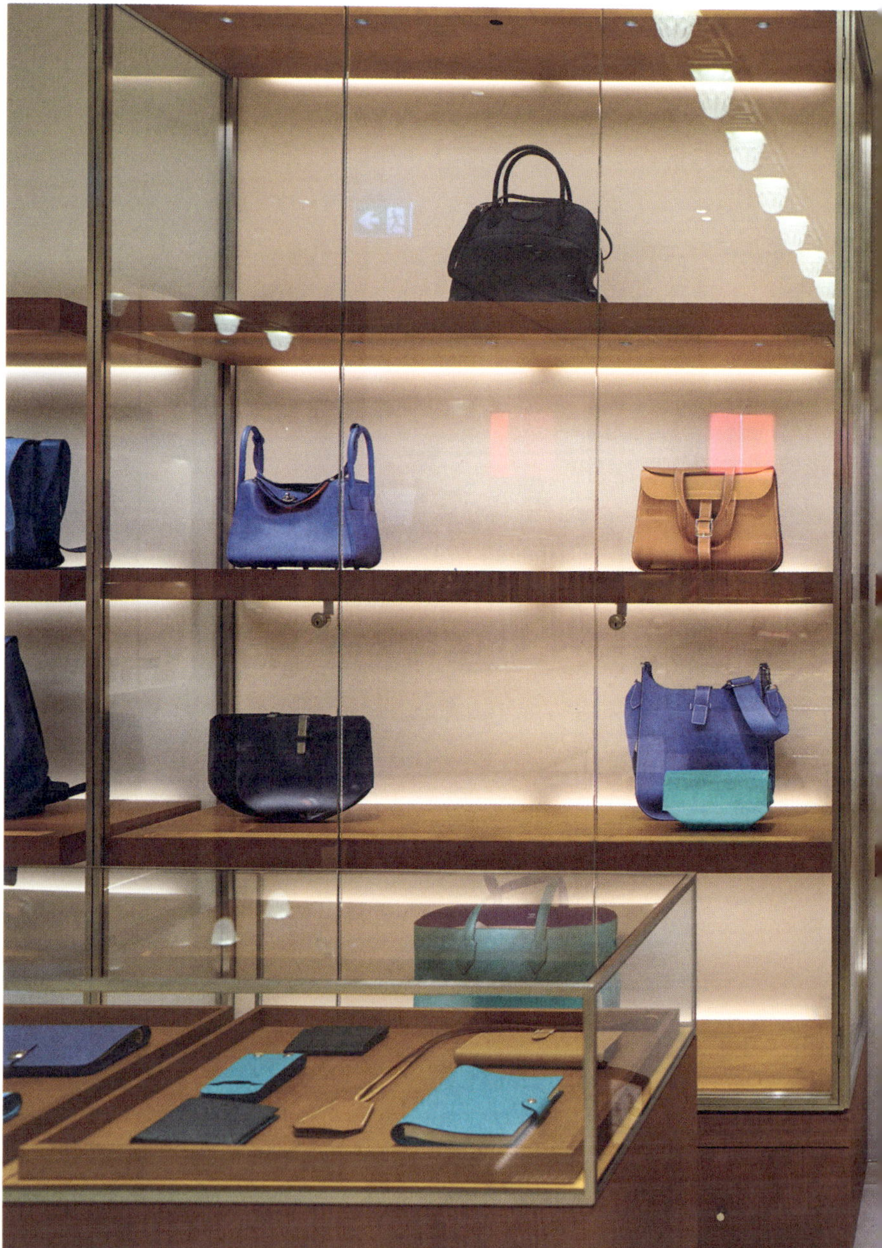

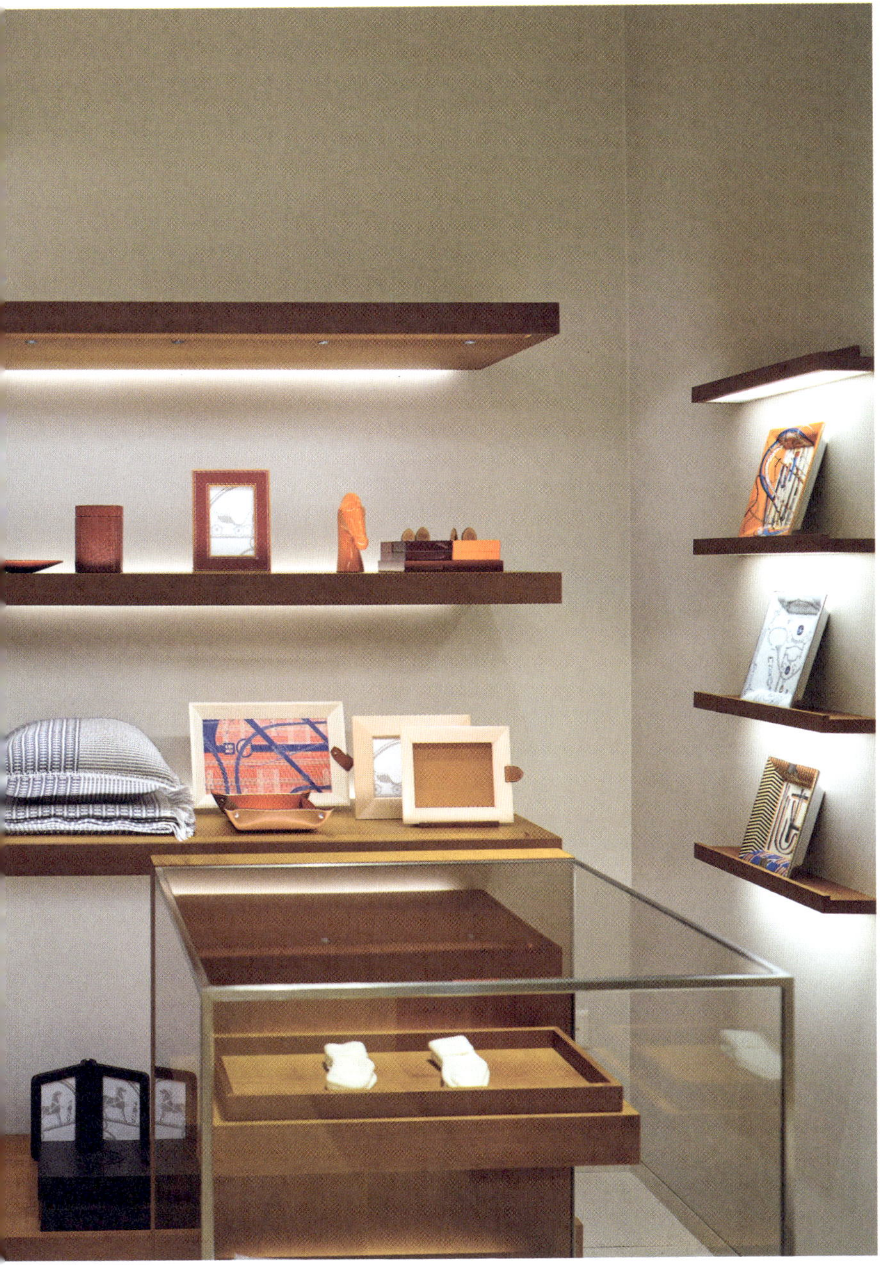

Other *HERMÈS HANDBAGS*

Even though it might seem that Hermès is just known for making the Birkin and Kelly bags, they do have a variety of handbags and leather goods that are easier to get your hands on. Today, there are 17 different handbags in all shapes, sizes, and colors. Here are a few of the most popular.

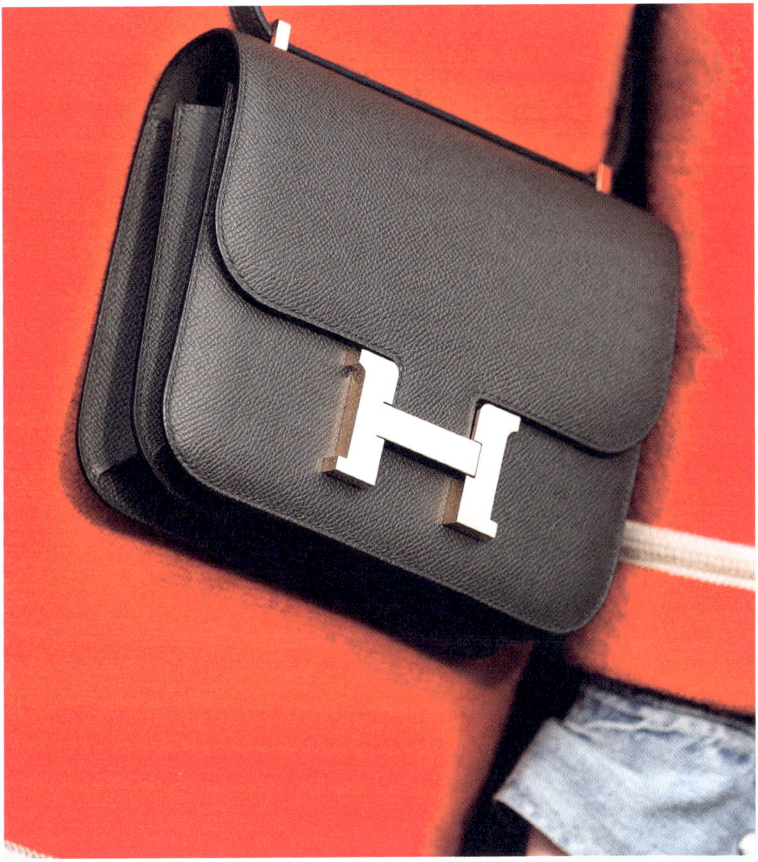

CONSTANCE BAG

A smaller, urban, and more casual bag than some of the others that Hermès makes, the Constance bag was created in 1967. The designer named it after her daughter. It comes in different sizes, but it's a basic flap bag with the "H" logo in different hardware on the front that is actually the clasp for the bag. The Constance is a clever design that can be worn crossbody or as a shoulder bag.

LINDY BAG

The Lindy Bag is a slouchy, supple bag that can be worn crossbody in three different sizes: mini, 26, and 34. It also has handles on the sides instead of at the top, making this a unique design choice. Out of all the Hermès bags, it's the least structured and most casual. The iconic turn clasp is definitely a Hermès signature. This bag was designed by Jean-Paul Gaultier and came out in 2007. This is the kind of bag that would be the perfect gift for a high school or college grad for a first Hermès bag.

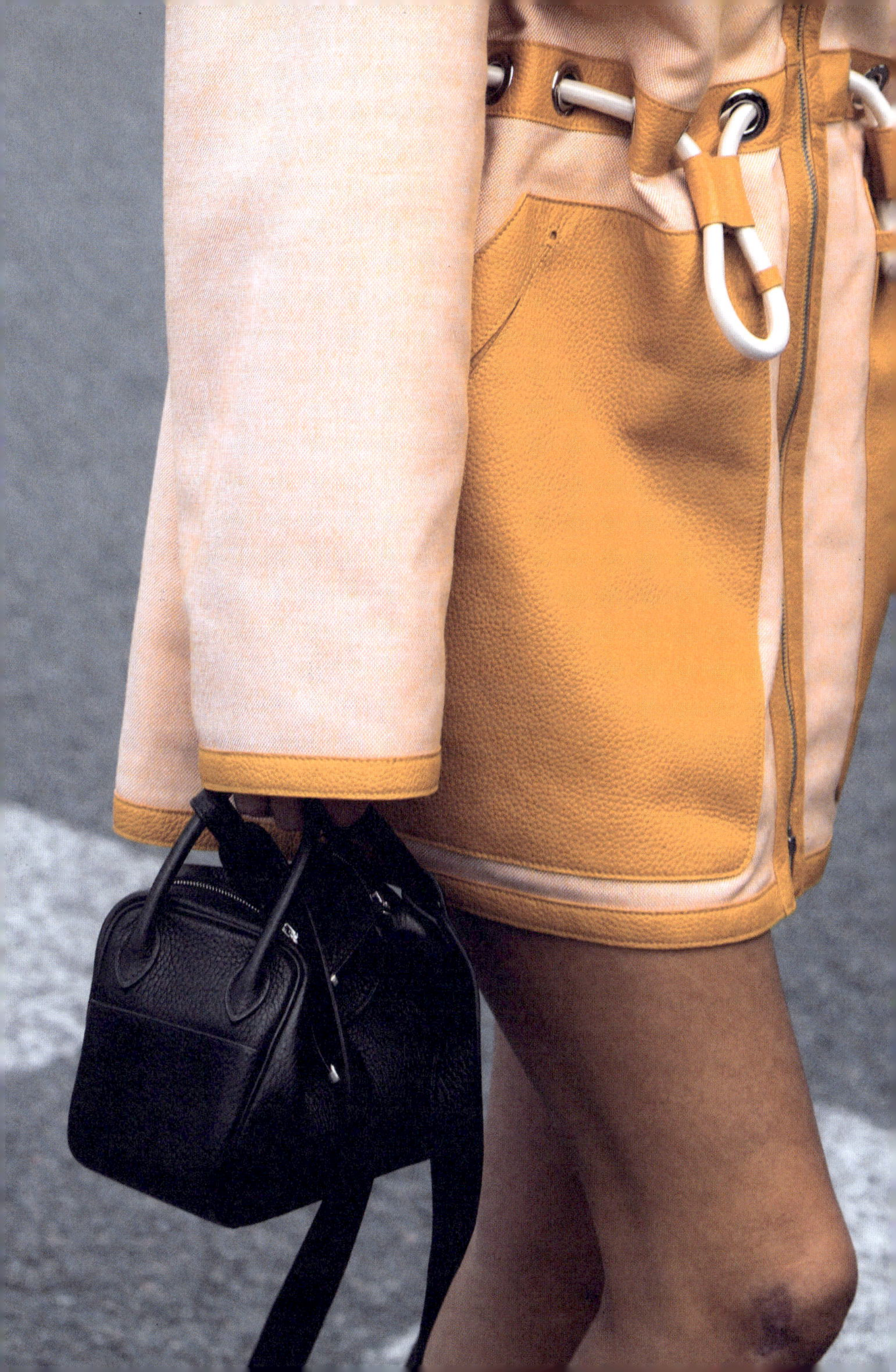

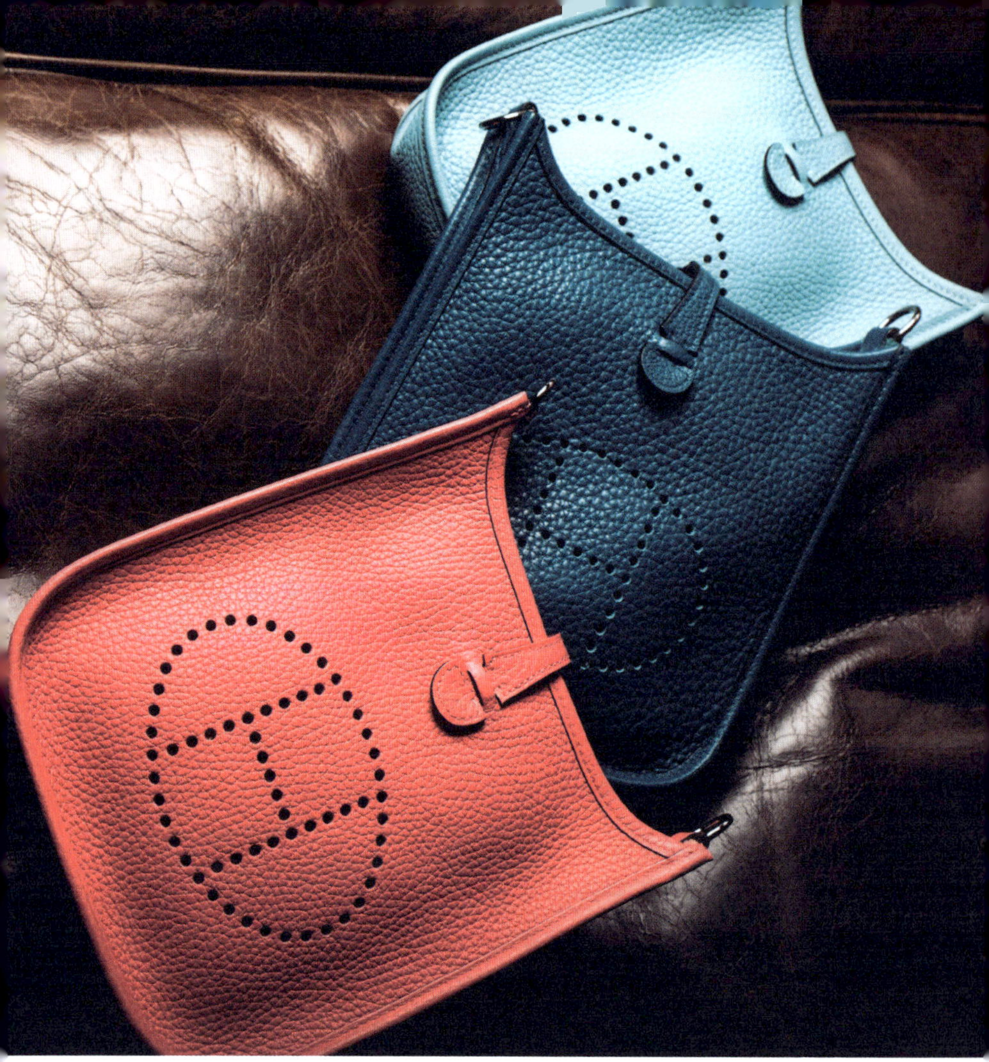

EVELYNE BAG

This is a historic bag that came out in 1978. It was designed by the head of the Hermès riding department, Evelyne Bertrand. The goal of the bag was to carry the tools of a horse groomer, but today Gen Z loves it because it has the H logo in perforated cut-out on the front of the bag in the leather. As an easy-to-carry crossbody bag, this casual style is truly meant to throw in your wallet, smartphone, lipstick, and keys and go. Three different sizes make this bag perfect in functionality, with tons of different color options and printed straps.

GARDEN PARTY BAG

Released in 1964, this popular tote bag quickly became a big hit for Hermès. It comes in three different sizes, but the largest one is ideal for a weekend getaway bag. The bag is pretty simple in style, but it's just gorgeous, with plunging handles and "Clou de Selle" buttons that secure the bag closed. This genius tote works in the city, in the Hamptons, or pretty much anywhere you want to go.

VERROU BAG

This ladylike bag has a complex slide clasp that is made of 25 pieces, inspired by a horse stall latch. The equestrian heritage of Hermès is alive and well in this beautiful bag that came out with an updated version in 2010. The original Verrou was more of a clutch or pochette. The straps vary on this bag from a jeweled chain to leather, depending on which style you choose. It comes in two sizes, a mini and a Verrou 21, which is a medium-sized shoulder or cross-body bag.

"HERMÈS IS THE EPITOME OF *LUXURY AND SOPHISTICATION.* ITS ICONIC DESIGNS STAND THE TEST OF TIME, REPRESENTING THE ULTIMATE IN *ELEGANCE AND QUALITY.*"

Tyra Banks

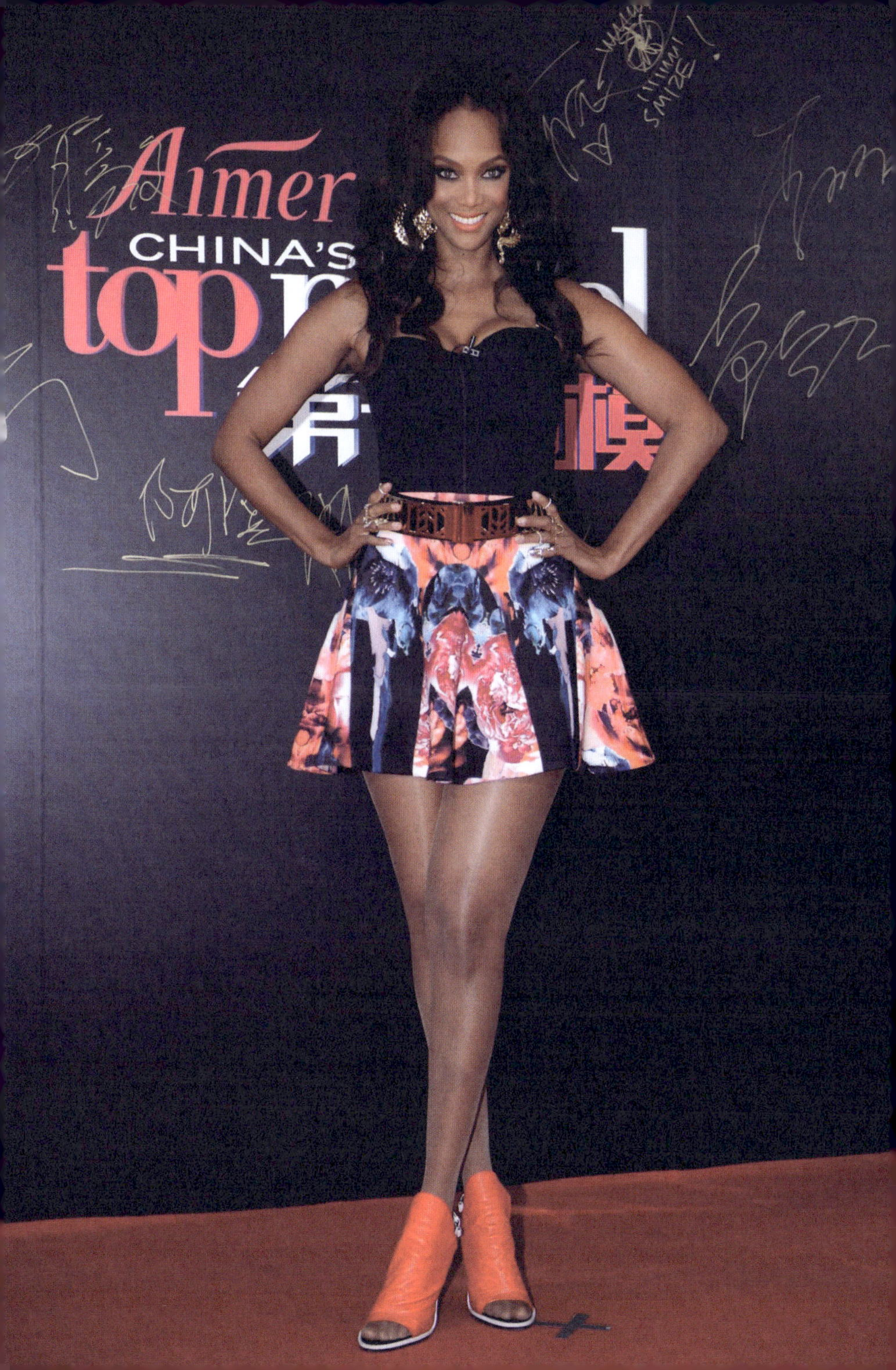
Aimer
CHINA'S
top

7

HERMÈS FRAGRANCE and NEW MAKEUP

Fragrance

GREAT FRAGRANCES AND MAKEUP always have a significant place in pop culture. When these products come from a luxury fashion house, they become a force of power and prestige. Hermès has a long history of putting out amazing fragrances, but makeup is relatively new for the historic luxury brand.

The first Hermès fragrance came out in 1951, called Eau d'Hermès. It's still made by the brand today and is consistently one of its best sellers. Edmond Roudnitska was the perfumer who created this lush and spicy citrus/floral fragrance with notes of bergamot, lavender, jasmine, and leather. Men and women love this fragrance: It has a definite unisex appeal. The reason the base note is leather was in honor of the leather goods and handbags that Hermès created. They have released many fragrances over the years. Here are some of the most popular, along with the fragrance notes that have made these perfumes some of the best in the world for both men and women.

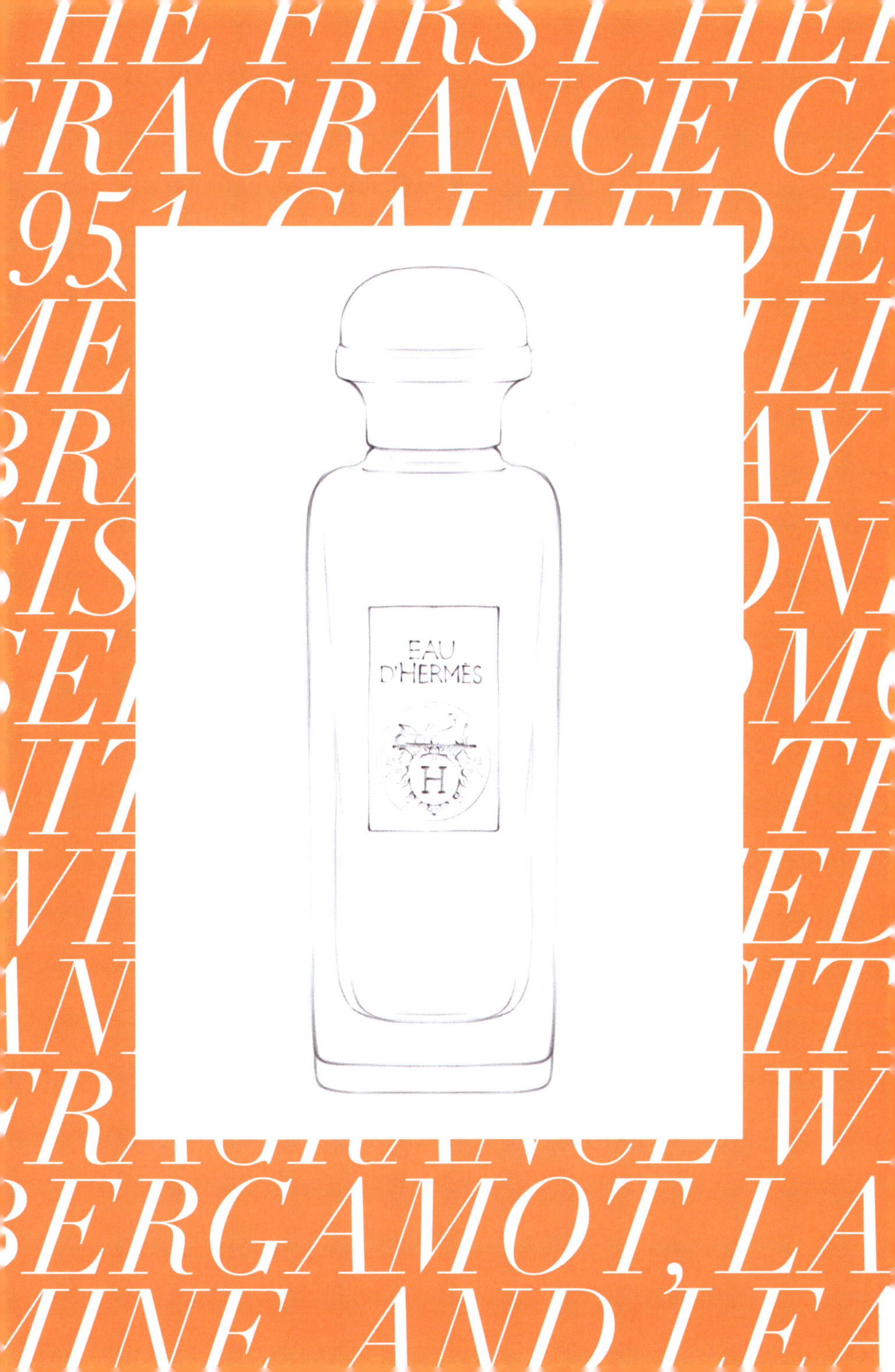
HE FIRST HER
RAGRANCE CA
EAU
D'HERMÈS
H
BERGAMOT, LA
MINE AND LEA

WOMEN'S FRAGRANCES

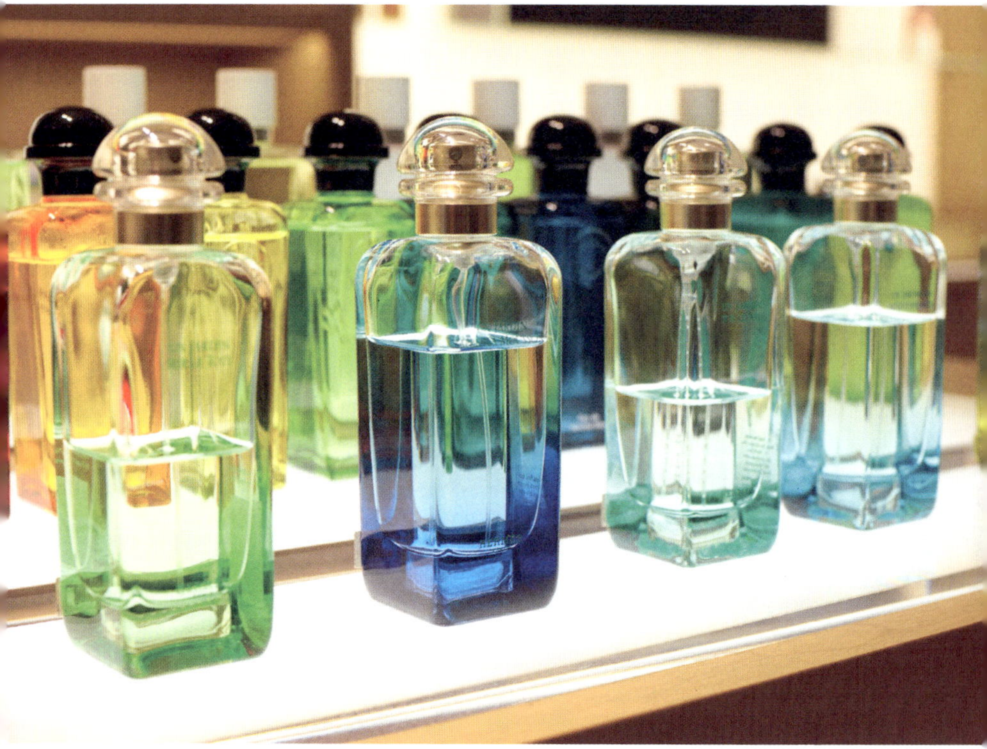

UN JARDIN *EN MEDITERRANEE*

This was created as part of a garden perfume line in 2003. Un Jardin en Mediterranee was the first of the floral-inspired collection that was released. The goal when wearing this is to picture yourself walking through a Tunisian garden with trees and flowers blowing in the breeze. With woody undertones, fig, and soft floral oleander, this is a fragrance that feels like a fresh spring day. The bottle is unique, inspired by the lines of a lantern on a horse-drawn carriage.

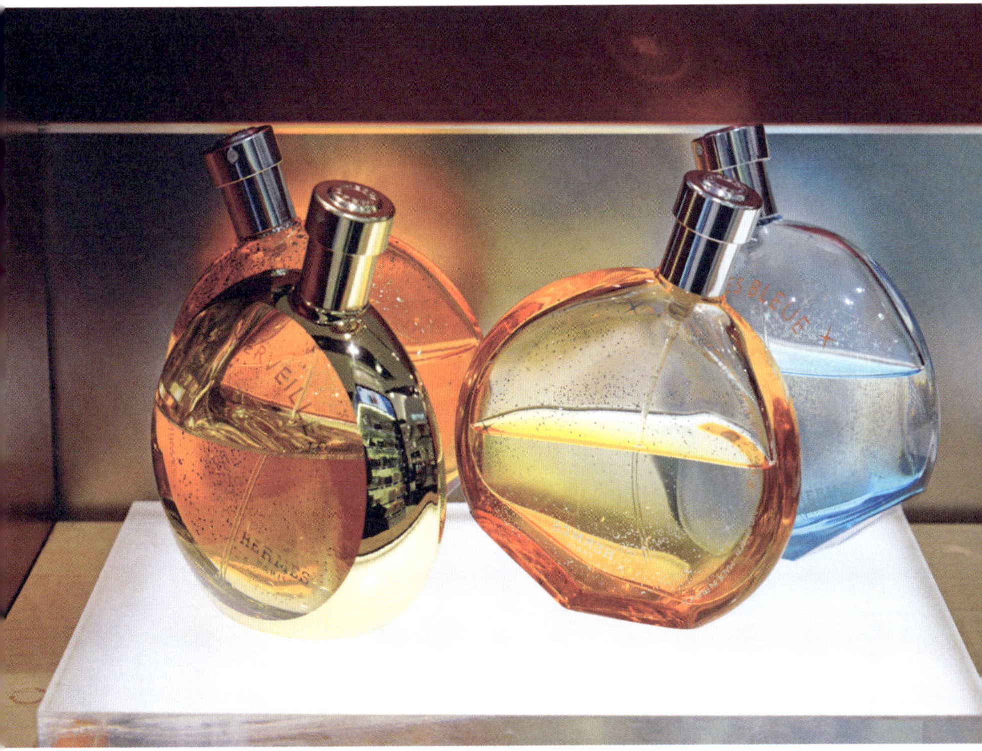

EAU DES *MERVEILLES*

In 2004, Hermès created a completely different fragrance for the line. Starting with the bottle, it's round. The name means "waters of wonders" and showcases ambergris as one of its main ingredients. The scent is ambery, warm, and spicy and has notes of orange blending seamlessly with benzoin that smells of leathery vanilla. A totally unique scent that people practically become addicted to.

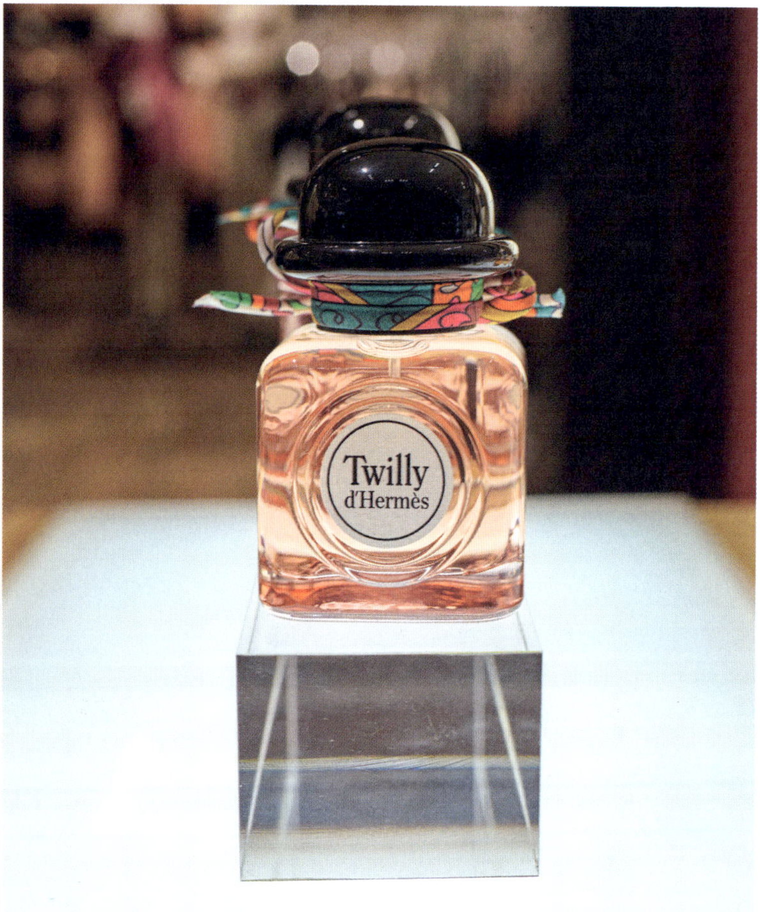

TWILLY, *DE HERMÈS*

A fun fragrance that just came out in 2017, Twilly de Hermès is meant to cater to the younger Hermès lover. The Twilly is, of course, the smaller scarf or hair tie that is meant to be collectible as a smaller format of the iconic scarf. The fragrance bottle even comes with a tiny Twilly that is tied around its neck; It has a black top, and the liquid is pink. The scent is youthful energy with notes of ginger, tuberose, and bitter orange. Vanilla rounds out the bottom of this jazzy floral fragrance.

24 FAUBOURG

This fragrance is named for the street of Hermès' flagship store in Paris on the Rue Faubourg. It came out in 1995, so the scent of this is sunny and bright with amber and floral notes. Orange blossom, jasmine, and vanilla blend perfectly in this classic scent with a bottle design that is inspired by a Hermès scarf blowing in a gentle breeze. Elegant and luminous, once you start wearing 24 Faubourg, you'll love it forever.

KELLY *CALECHE*

Caleche is a French word meaning "single-horse carriage." And Kelly is obviously named for the famous Kelly bag. So Kelly Caleche is a fragrance that came out in 2007 as an ode to these two iconic symbols for Hermès. The scent of this fragrance is chypre floral with notes of grapefruit, lily of the valley, rose, and powdery mimosa. Discreet notes of leather run through the base of the fragrance, obviously in honor of the handbag as well as the leather reins on a horse-drawn carriage. There was an older fragrance called Caleche that came out in 1961: It's one of their best sellers over the years, and it's still available in an eau de toilette.

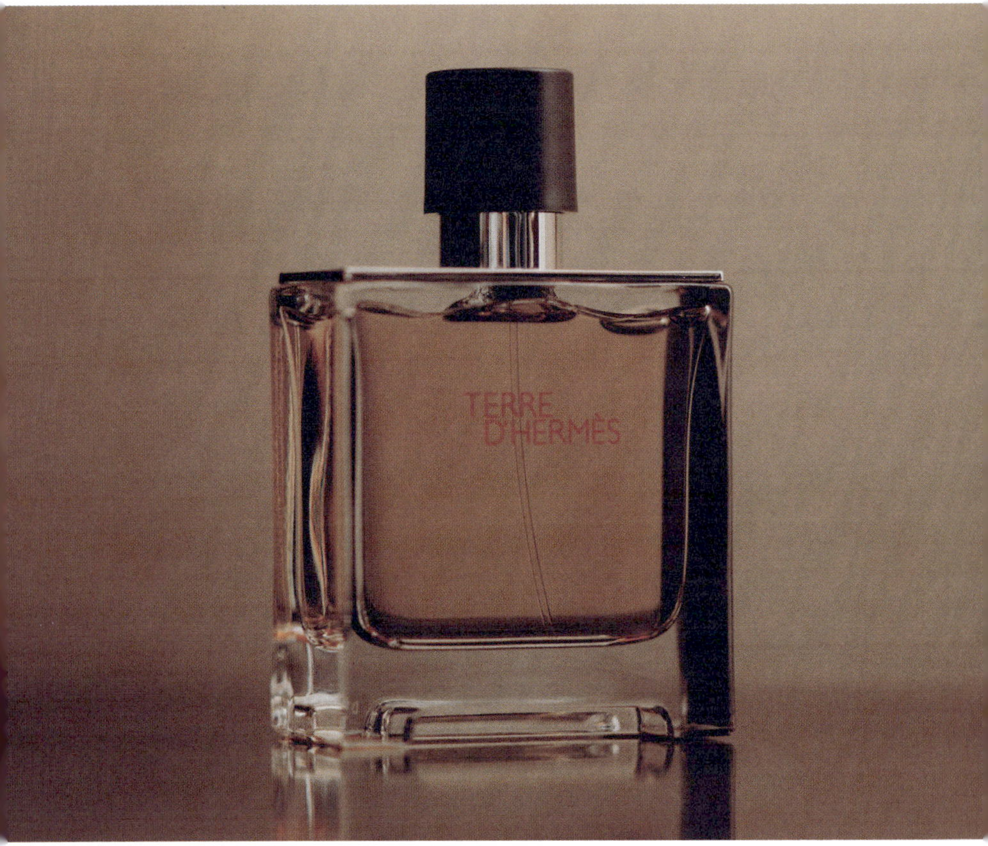

TERRE, *D'HERMÈS*

Released in 2006, Terre d'Hermès is a classic men's fragrance that is citrusy and woody. The notes are orange, pepper, vetiver, and cedar. You can practically smell the men's locker room at any upscale gym when you catch of whiff of this cologne. It's been very successful for Hermès and won a coveted Fifi Award for "Fragrance of the Year" in 2007.

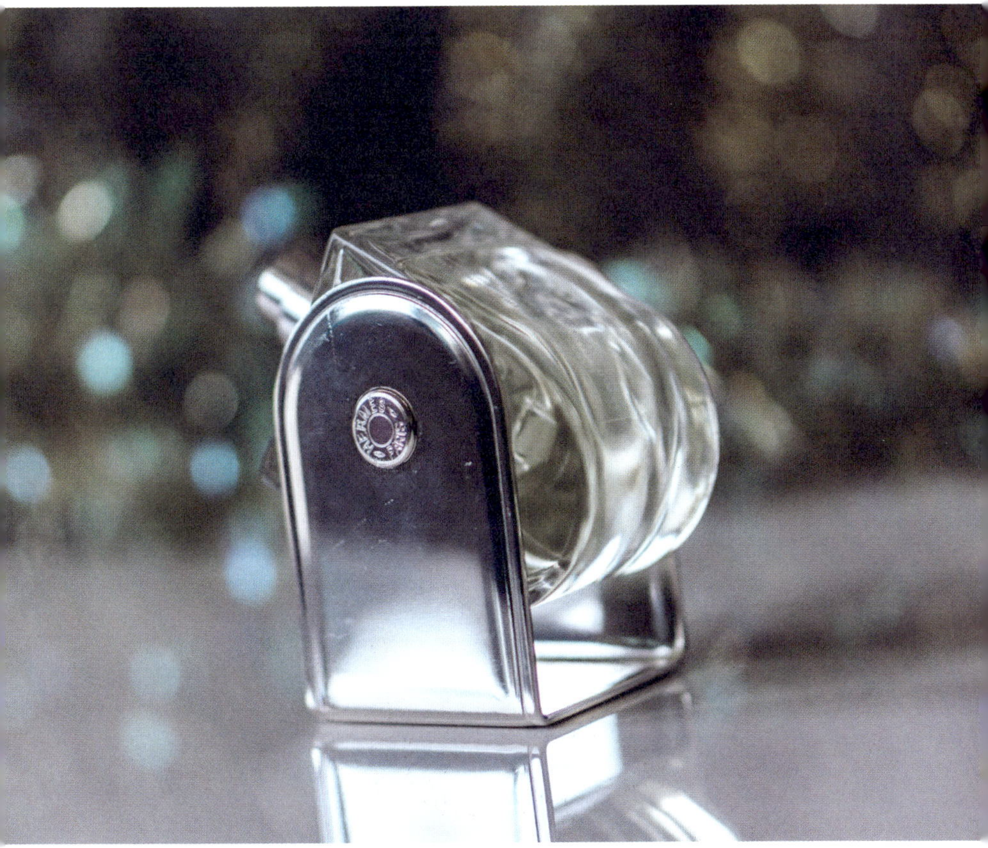

VOYAGE *D'HERMÈS*

A few years later, Hermès wanted to capture magic in a bottle again with the creation of Voyage d'Hermès in 2010. It's a woody, floral musk that is layered with notes of juniper berry and milky sandalwood. A warm and sensual fragrance, it has a bottle inspired by a magnifying glass, with the famous Clou de Selle button from Hermès in the center of the bottle.

HERMÈS BEAUTY

Makeup is relatively new for Hermès, starting in 2020. They have never done makeup before, so they started out small, with just a line of 24 matte- and satin-finish lipsticks. The line of lipsticks is called Rouge Hermès, after a fragrance collection that came out in 2000. The lipsticks are meant to be inspired by the famous Birkin bag, with the matte texture being similar to the supple leather that the iconic handbags are made of. The colors of the lipstick were matched with some of the leather and silk samples for the scarves that Hermès has created over the decades.

The cases are tricolored, different for each lipstick, and designed by Pierre Hardy, who is the creative director of jewelry and shoes. Today, they offer more lipstick shades, with each one being refillable. They even come out with limited-edition colors each season, as well as sets where you can customize which three lipsticks you would like to own. The lipsticks on their own are like tiny works of art, but that's not all that Hermès Beauty offers today. Here are some other cosmetic items that have the beauty and heritage of this iconic line behind them.

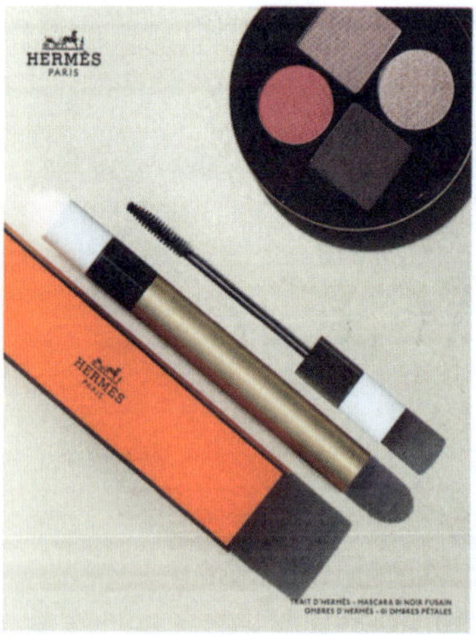

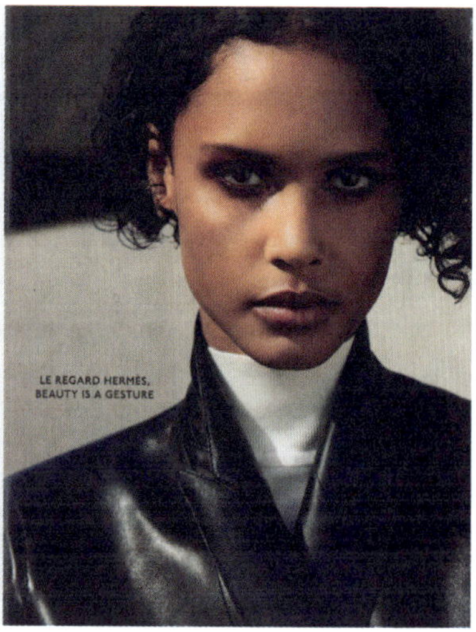

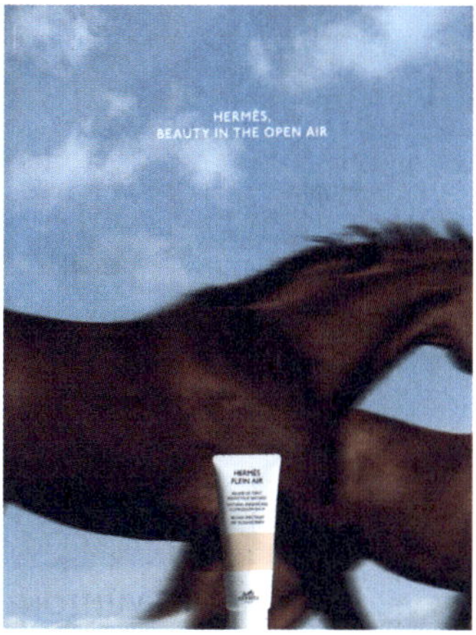

HERMÈS PLEIN AIR *COMPLEXION BALM*

A sheer weight foundation that comes in 12 different shades, the Hermès Plein Air Complexion Balm is natural-looking skin perfection. The finish is meant to last for eight hours, with natural ingredients such as green tea and evening primrose extract. It also has SPF 30 to keep your skin protected from the UVA/UVB rays of the sun. For $90, skin better look absolutely flawless using a tube of this beauty balm.

HERMESISTIBLE *INFUSED CARE OIL*

Everyone loves lip gloss. Hermès jumped into this one with its Hermesistible Infused Care Oil. In bright washes of color, the lip oil is glossy perfection. In five different shades, such as Rose Pitaya, Beige Sapotille, and Pourpre Camarine, which is a deep purple, each one is meant to hydrate and nourish, with 97 percent natural ingredients. The most unique thing about these lip oils is that each has a different fruity scent, created by Christine Nagel, the Hermès head perfumer.

“HERMÈS EMBODIES THE EPITOME OF ELEGANCE AND STYLE.”

Camila Cabello

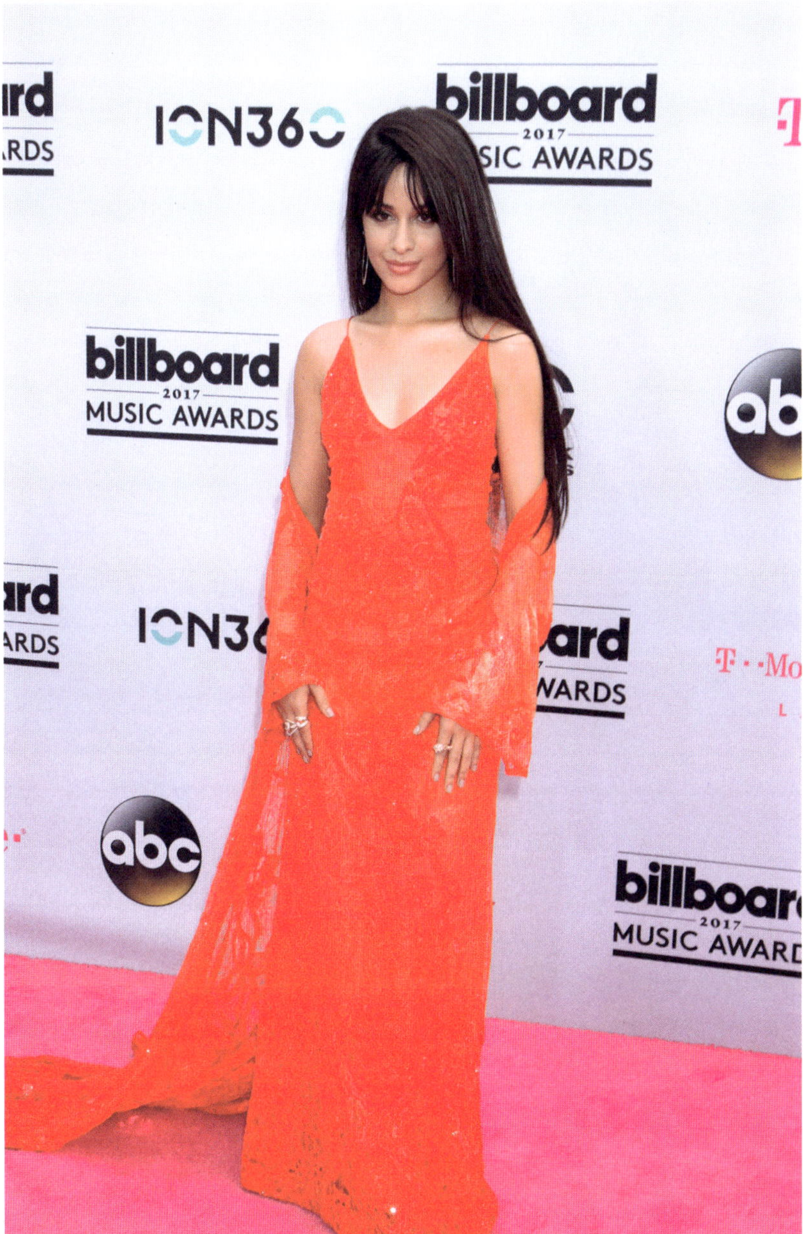
billboard
2017
MUSIC AWARDS
ION360
abc

8

HERMÈS *DOESN'T USE* AMBASSADORS

Advertising

HERE'S ANOTHER BIT OF INFORMATION ABOUT HERMÈS that makes them different than any other luxury fashion brand. They don't use ambassadors. Plain and simple. Hermès doesn't hire specific celebrities to be ambassadors. Other than Princess Grace Kelly being known for the Kelly bag and Jane Birkin's history of being the inspiration for the Birkin bag, the House of Hermès doesn't really look to models and celebrities to tote their products. Of course, they do use runway models to show each season's ready-to-wear clothing. Celebrities, politicians, and royalty pretty much wear, buy, and are given all kinds of Hermès items.

The idea with Hermès is that the brand's iconic appeal and storied history are enough to make it sought after. No celebs or models are necessary. Former CEO Jean-Louis Dumas once explained it perfectly: "We don't have a policy of image, we have a policy of product." Basically, he's saying that the brand's philosophy is that the products are good enough to stand on their own.

Tons of other brands, such as Gucci, Dior, Chanel, and Louis Vuitton, actively go after being represented and worn by certain popular celebrities. Hermès is able to be just as popular but flies a bit under the radar. The brand certainly doesn't need anyone's celebrity endorsement to be successful. Many people still crave their products, especially the famous Birkin and Kelly bags, and spend years on the waiting list. How wild is that?

HE IDEA WIT
THAT THE BRA

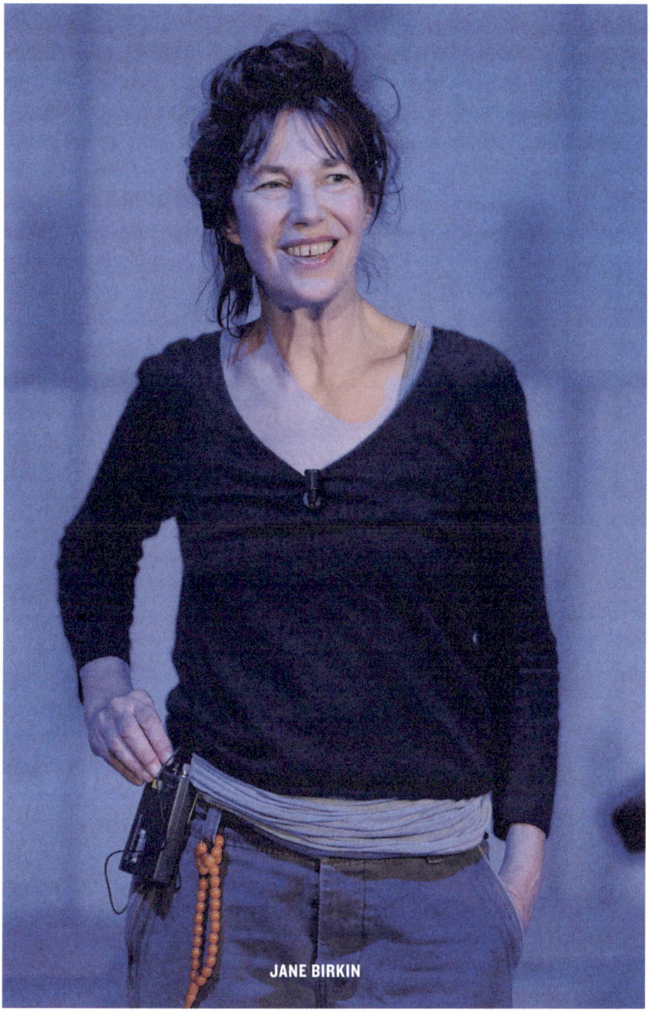
JANE BIRKIN

CY OF PRÓDUC
HE'S SAYING T

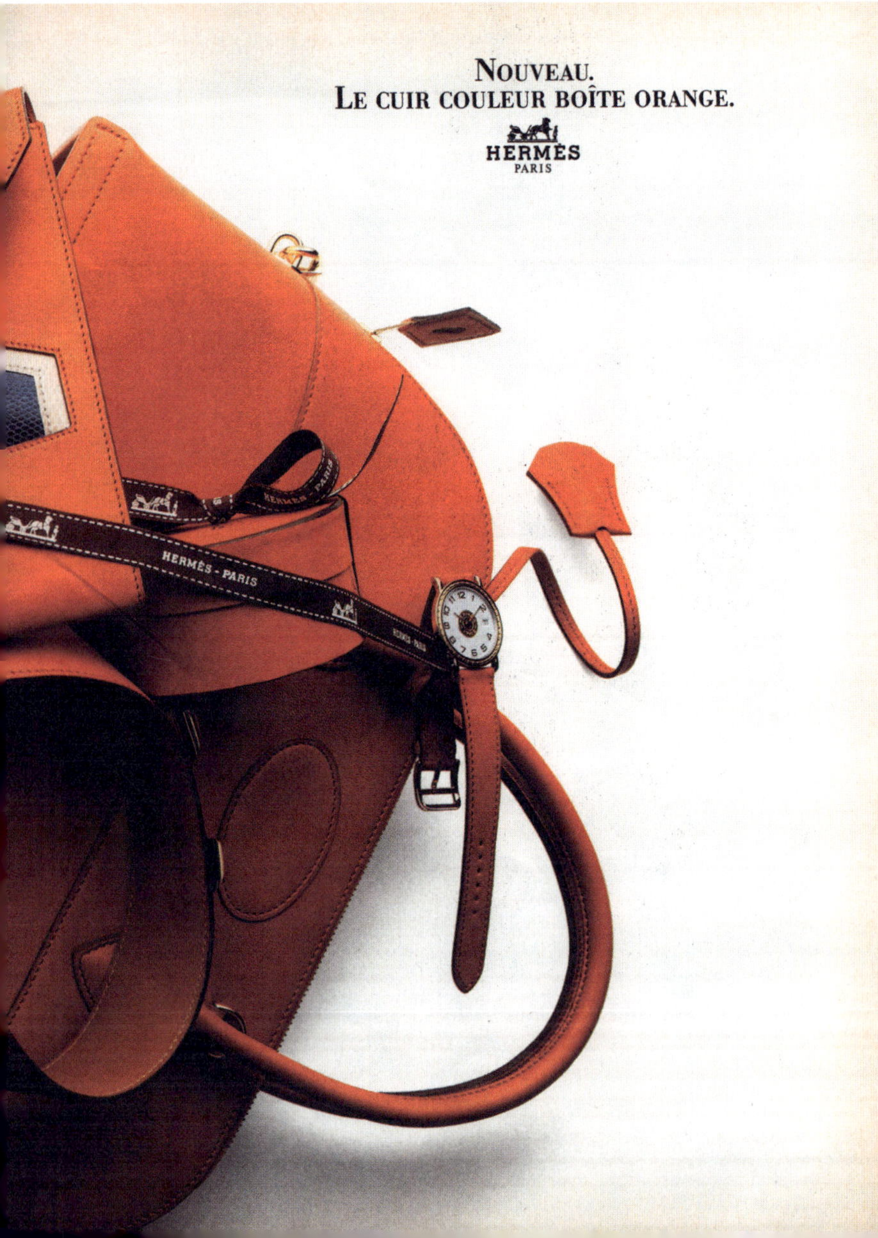
NOUVEAU.
LE CUIR COULEUR BOÎTE ORANGE.
HERMÈS
PARIS
HERMÈS - PARIS

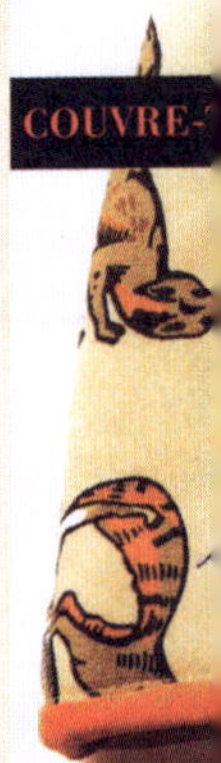
COUVRE-

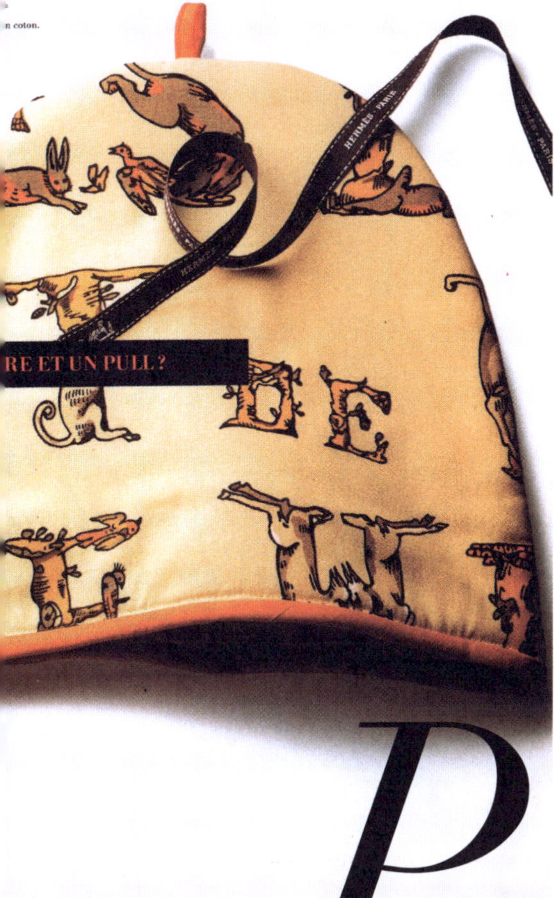

PRODUCT FOCUS
Hermès does not use ambassadors, so it is often the products and not models that are the focus when the brand markets its products.

Plus, Hermès is still one of the only luxury brands that is still majority family owned to this day. They haven't been acquired by bigger luxury conglomerates, such as LVMH, Kering, Richemont, or the Luxottica Group. It speaks to the endurance of the brand and the strong family values behind it.

They also don't do "collabs" with celebrities or popular designers, as many luxury fashion houses do. Think of Rihanna with Puma, Beyonce with Balmain, Gigi Hadid with Tommy Hilfiger, or Celeste with Dior. Hermès just isn't interested in that. The fact is that with all of the success they have had for almost 200 years, they just don't need anyone's endorsement.

"HERMÈS REPRESENTS THE EPITOME OF LUXURY AND CRAFTSMAN-SHIP."

Jennifer Lopez

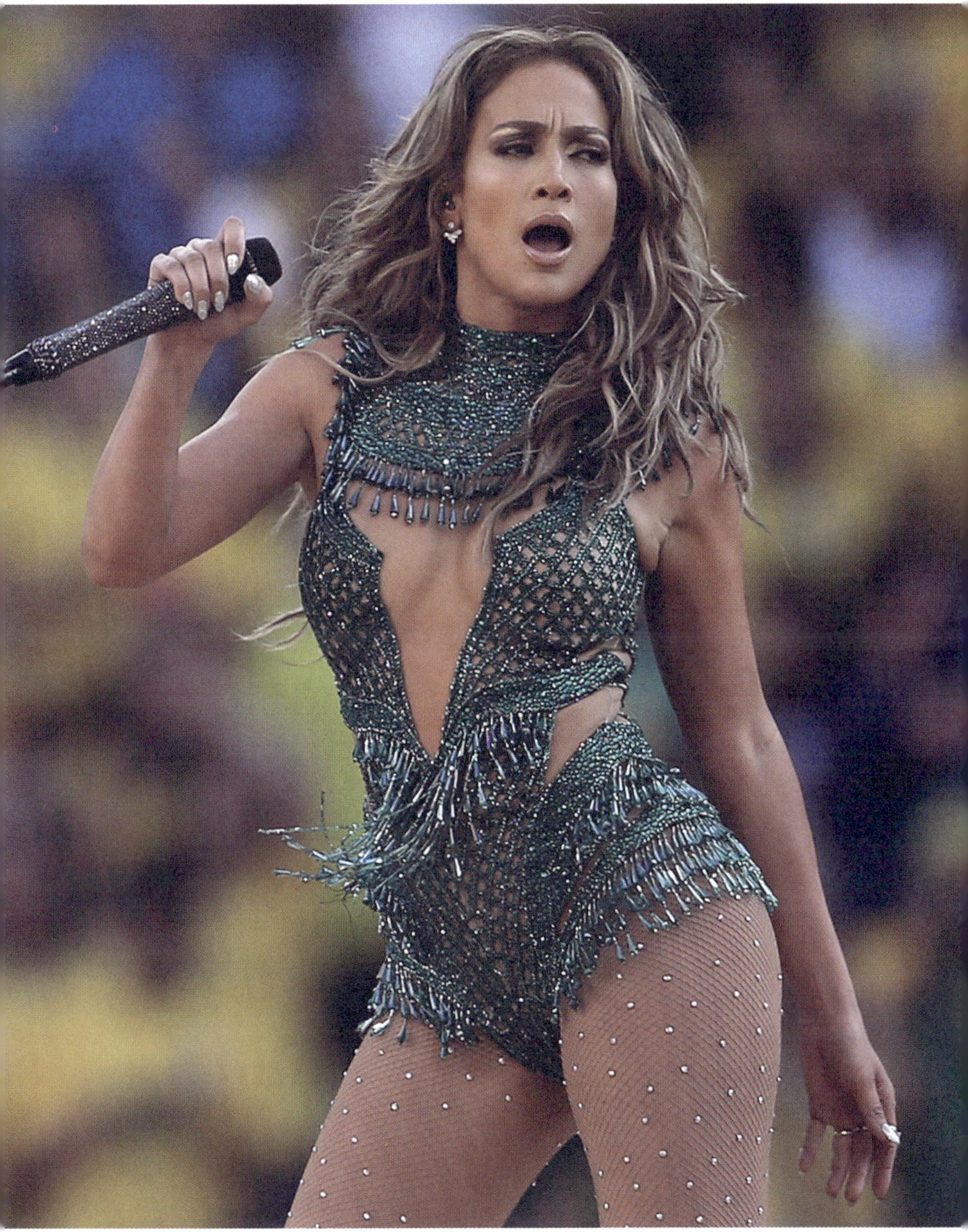

9

CELEBS *WHO CARRY THE* BIRKIN *or* KELLY BAG

Celebrities

WANT TO HEAR A CRAZY STATISTIC about the Birkin bag?

HIGHEST QUALITY
Handcraftsmanship remains paramount at Hermès, which uses the finest materials to produce scarves, bags, and much more.

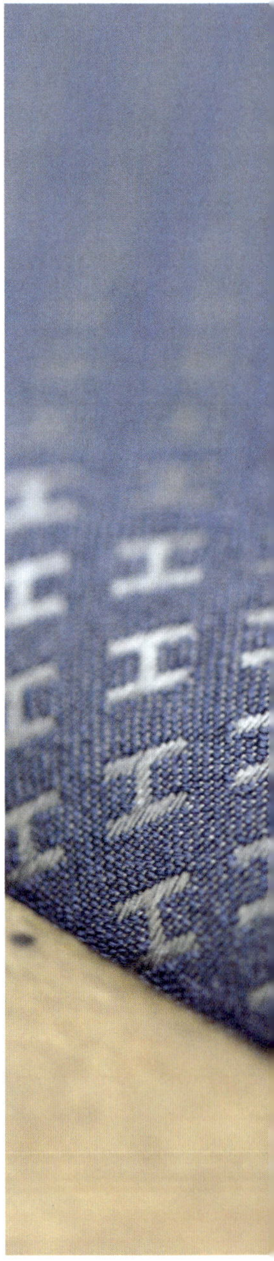

It's crafted by a single artisan and takes at least 25 hours to make. The Kelly bag is a little bit smaller, so it takes around 20 hours to complete. The craftsmanship needed for each of these bags makes it an actual work of art. Maybe that's why the continued popularity and allure creates an end product that is so special. Coveted. Desired. Lusted after. Even though the price of a Birkin or Kelly bag can go for hundreds of thousands of dollars. Ashton Kutcher once said, "I learned what a Birkin bag is from the price tag. You'll never forget what it is once you've paid for one."

That's why celebrities, politicians, and royalty have amassed quite a collection that they are regularly seen with. So who is carrying a Birkin or Kelly bag currently? Or who has been seen with one throughout the decades? Here are some of the most famous people who adore their Hermès handbags.

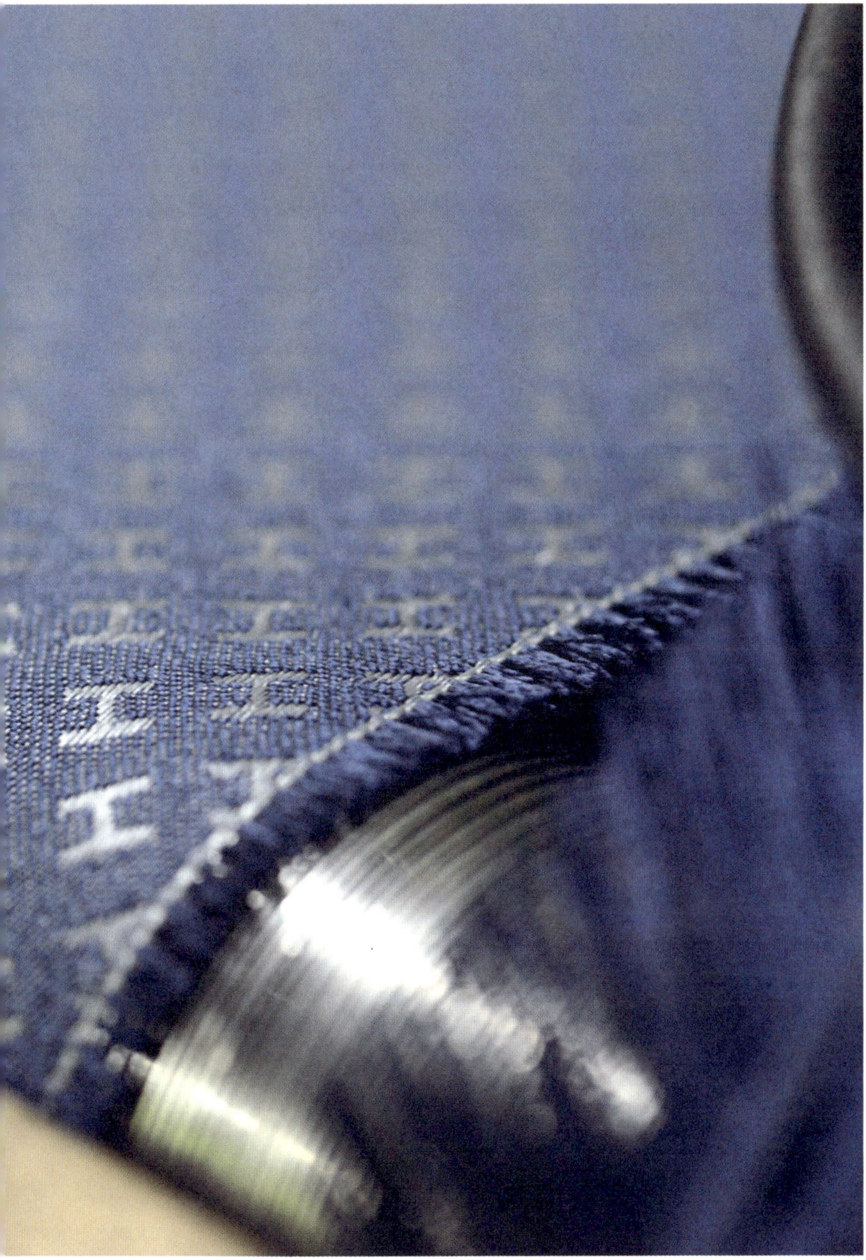

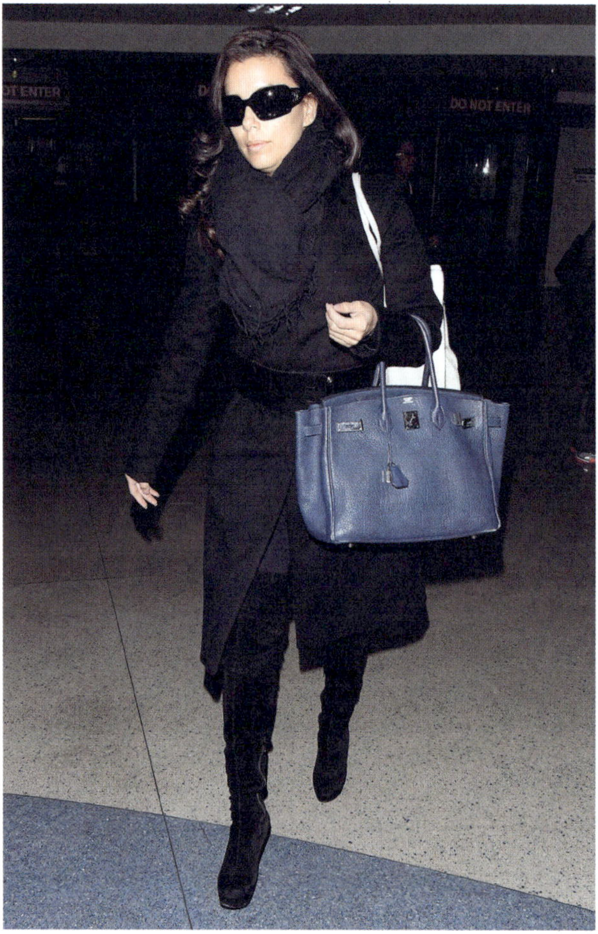

EVA LONGORIA

This actress has been photographed with several Birkins over the years. That includes ones in tan, dark brown, navy blue, black, and gray. The gray one is called Gris Tourterelle by Hermès, and it's kind of a cross between gray and beige, depending on the light. It seems like she's kept to the more neutral Birkin bags so that they go with everything. She also owns a reddish-brown Kelly bag. Lucky lady.

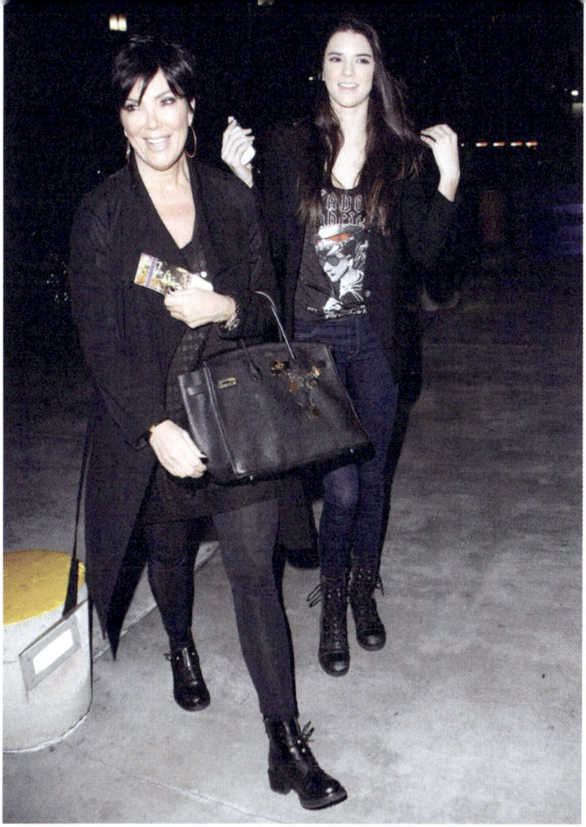

THE KARDASHIANS

We're just going to lump all the Kardashians into this category. Kim, Khloe, Kourtney, Kendall (Jenner), and Kylie (Jenner) all have been photographed with Birkin bags. Their love of Hermès is well known. Even their mom, Kris Jenner, is a die-hard Birkin fan. These women have some legendary bags. Kim, Khloe, and Kylie have all shown off some of their Birkin and Kelly collections on social media. Kim's collection is especially enormous, featuring practically every style and size of Birkin imaginable. The most valuable one she has is a rare Himalayan Birkin, which is made of white crocodile exotic skin and goes for around $100,000. Kylie and Kris each own a Himalayan Birkin as well.

Khloe once posted a picture of her young daughter, True, surrounded by her collection of Birkin bags, which numbered 14 bags in the picture. Kendall is usually a little more low key than her sisters, but she's definitely into the Birkin as well. She's been photographed with a black mini Birkin and the largest Birkin, the 45, in both black and tan.

JENNIFER LOPEZ

Jenny from the Block, J-Lo, or Mrs. Ben Affleck certainly didn't grow up in the Bronx carrying a Birkin. She's made up for it in adulthood with all her success as an actress and singer, so she has quite a collection of handbags. Let's go right to the big one. She owns a Himalayan Niloticus Birkin bag that is worth a whopping $500,000. The hardware on the bag features 18ct white gold encrusted with diamonds. Wow. Just wow. Over the years, she's been photographed with at least 10 different Birkin bags. If you added up her entire collection, it would be worth several million dollars.

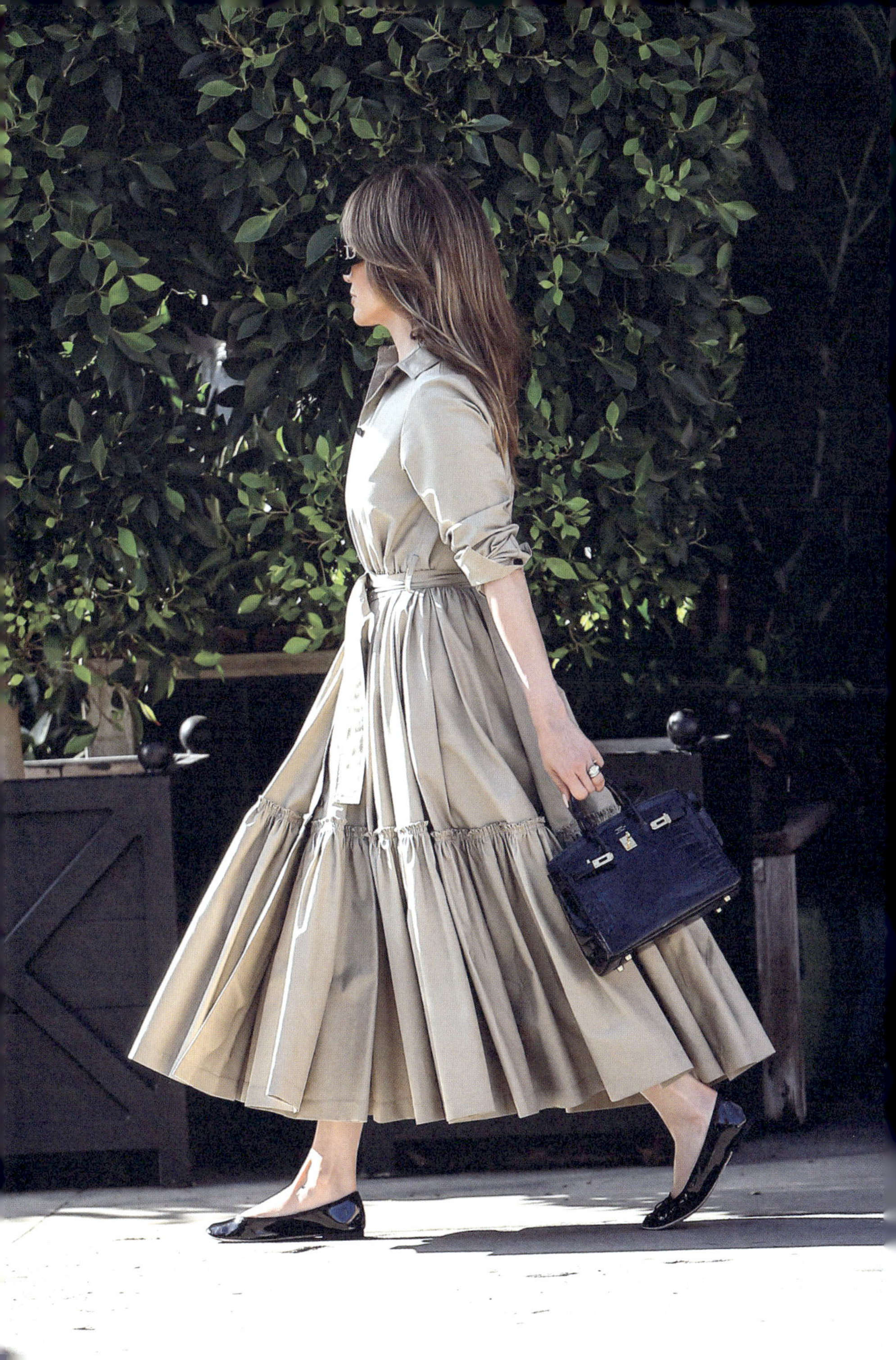

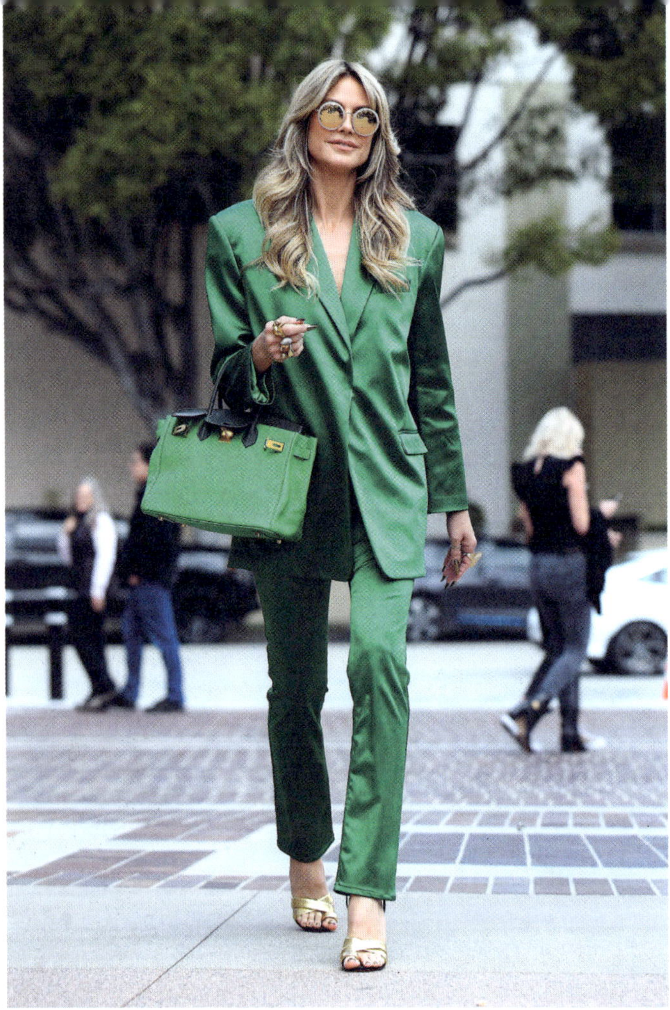

HEIDI KLUM

Supermodel Heidi Klum owns many Birkin bags. The one she is photographed with the most is a sky-blue Birkin bag. She also has a bright yellow Birkin 40 that's estimated to be worth almost $30,000. At least she's willing to experiment with color. Other times it's been a lime green or pink Birkin. The pink one is actually a Rose Pourpre ostrich exotic material in a 30cm size with palladium hardware. So chic.

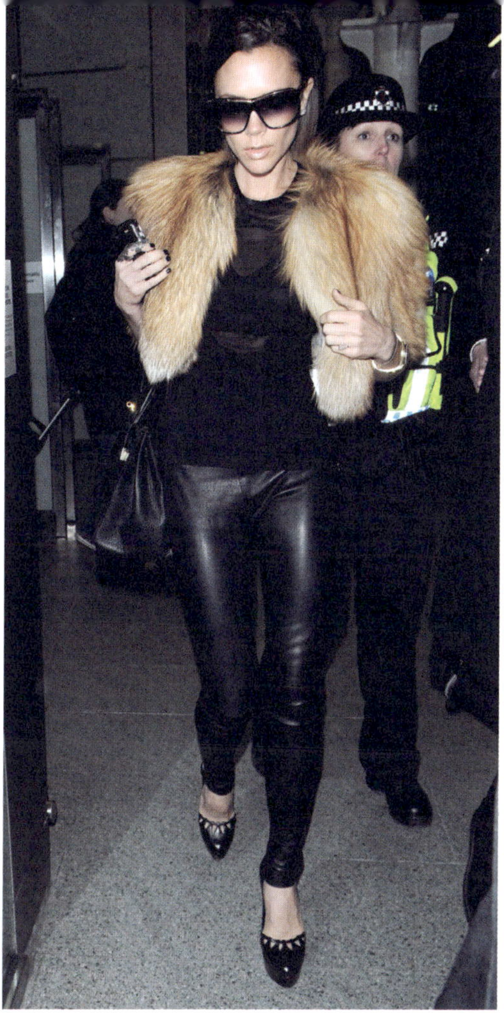

VICTORIA BECKHAM

The former Posh Spice is a Kelly bag lover. She has quite a few in her collection, but one of the most notable ones is the violet-purple Kelly bag in Doblis suede. Or maybe the tricolor Kelly is the coolest? Or how about the Kelly Longue or pochette in lizard? No matter which Kelly she's carrying, it's an elegant and expensive look.

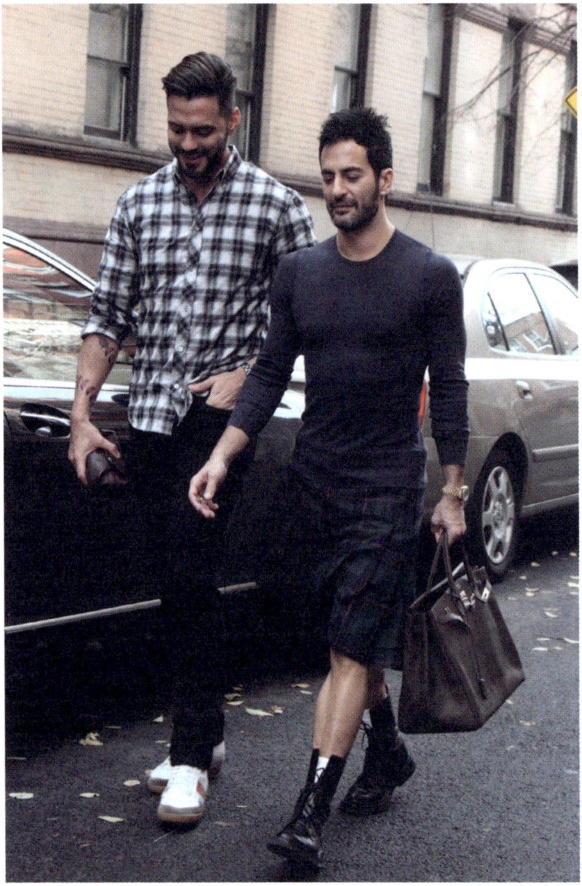

MARC JACOBS

Designer Marc Jacobs, who makes high-end handbags for his own line, has a thing for the Birkin. He's been photographed with a large black Birkin many times, even taking it to the beach. The bag was stuffed full with a beach towel and other things at St. Barts. Can you imagine getting sand on a $50,000 handbag?

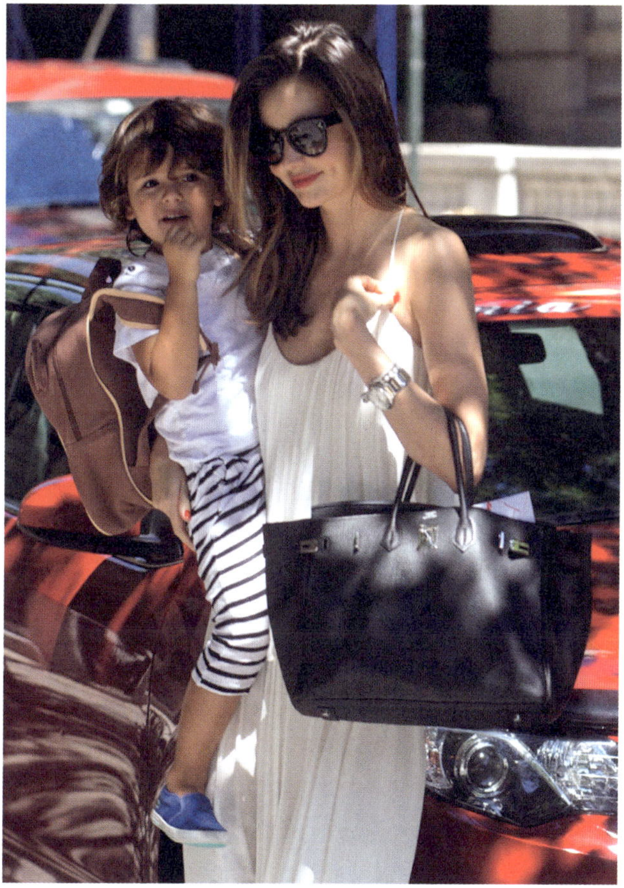

MIRANDA KERR

This supermodel and beauty mogul (she created Kora Cosmetics) has a collection of Kellys. Her taste is more understated, though, since most of the bags that she owns are in neutral colors. That doesn't make them any less special. That's just her style. She's been seen with a 32cm version of the Kelly in Etoupe Epsom leather that is the Sellier style in greige (gray beige) with gold hardware. It's a classic that will never go out of style.

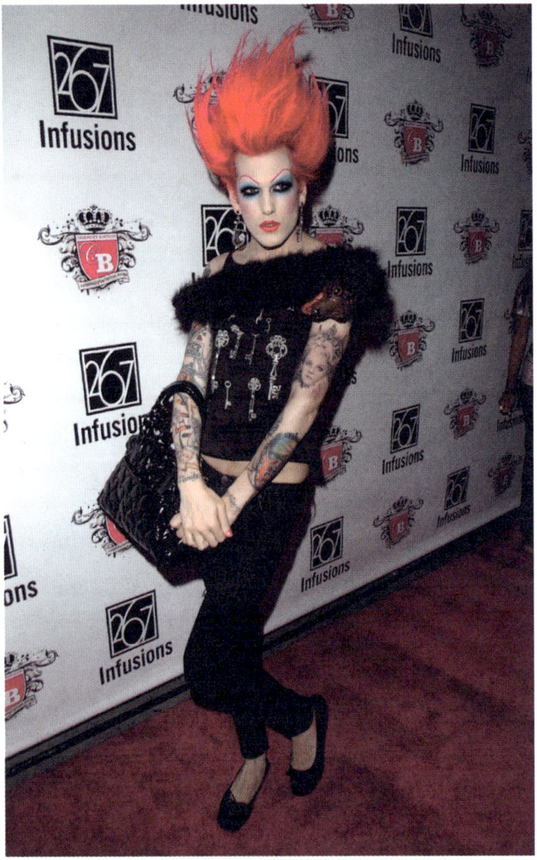

JEFFREE STAR

Internet personality and makeup artist Jeffree Star is a fan of the Kelly bag. He has a vault of candy-colored Hermès bags that is eye popping. That includes Birkins and Kellys galore. After showing off his closet full of goodies on YouTube, Jeffree claims that in 2022, he sold off his designer handbag collection for millions of dollars. Maybe after he had a Birkin stolen from his luggage on a flight from Scotland to LAX, he thought it was too big a burden to own such luxury. The one he lost was an ultra-rare $60,000 violet Birkin. He even posted on Twitter (now X) #PrayForTheBirkin. His prayers were answered. Three days after it went missing, the airline was able to find it and return it to him.

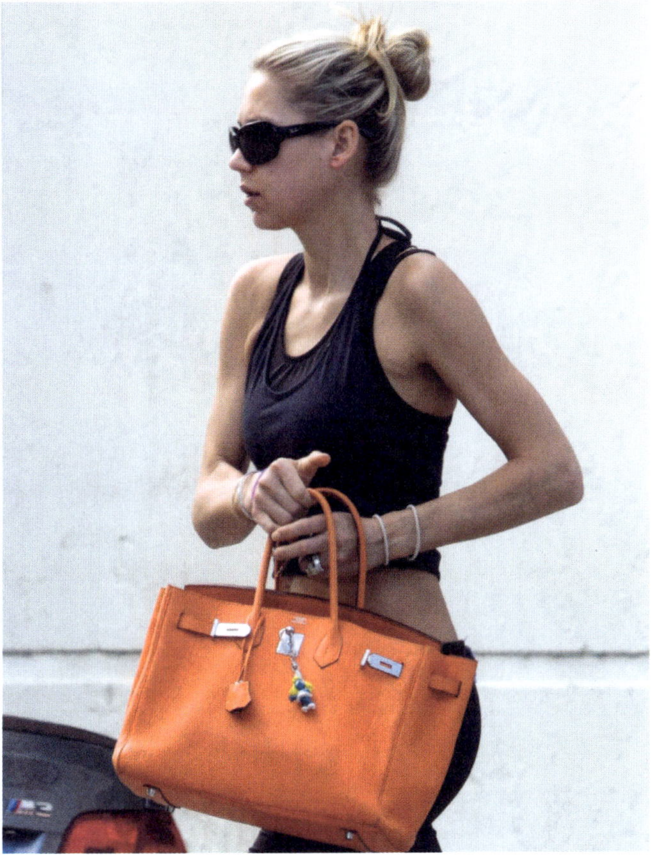

ANNA KOURNIKOVA

Anna Kournikova, the former tennis sensation, is frequently spotted carrying Birkin bags. Despite her tennis career being cut short due to injuries, the Russian athlete achieved a remarkable ranking of number eight in the world and secured two Grand Slam titles in doubles. On a personal note, Kournikova has been romantically linked with singer Enrique Iglesias since 2001 - coincidentally the year she starred in the music video for Iglesias' smash hit 'Escape'.

"HERMES REPRESENTS THE EPITOME OF TASTE AND REFINEMENT. IT'S NOT JUST ABOUT FASHION; IT'S ABOUT A LIFESTYLE."

David Beckham

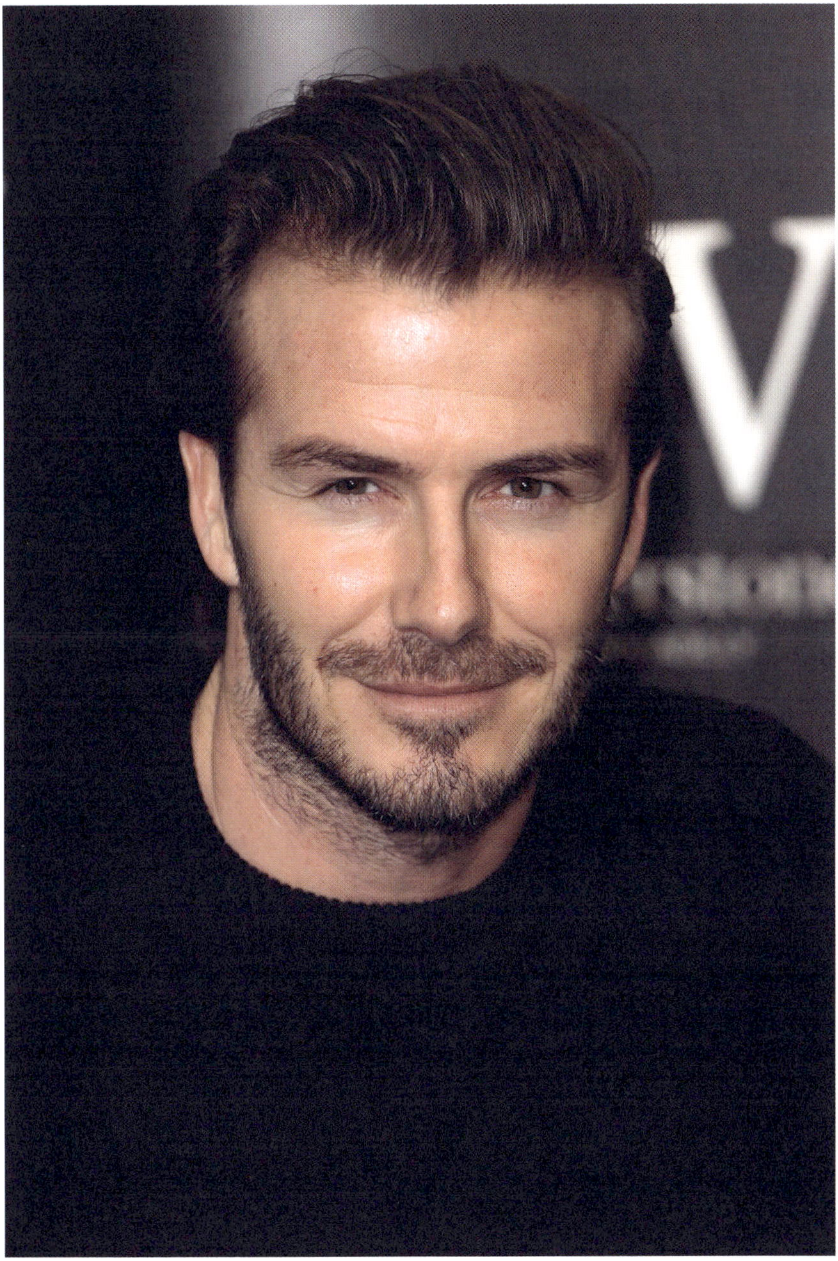

10

HERMÈS NOW *and* FOREVER

The Future

ON THE HERMÈS WEBSITE, the company describes itself as "contemporary artisans since 1837," and it's true. Everything they do is based on exceptional materials crafted by artists who really care about the luxury items they are making.

There is nothing mass produced about Hermès. When you own something from Hermès, you are buying a true piece of history from a family-owned company. Granted, that company is worth an estimated $247 billion, with annual sales in 2023 being around $13 billion. They have 300 stores in 45 different countries, employing 20,000 people. Each of these 300 stores is considered to have "houses for objects," so that each is like a mini museum of cherished items that anyone can own, with the right amount of cash or credit.

So what will the future of Hermès look like? Well, in basic terms, they will keep making gorgeous luxury pieces that everyone wants to own. Some of the main people involved in Hermès right now are creative director Nadège Vanhee-Cybulski and Axel Dumas, the CEO since 2014. Axel Dumas is a sixth-generation member of the Hermès-Dumas family. His uncle is Jean-Louis Dumas, who ran the company from 1978 to 2006.

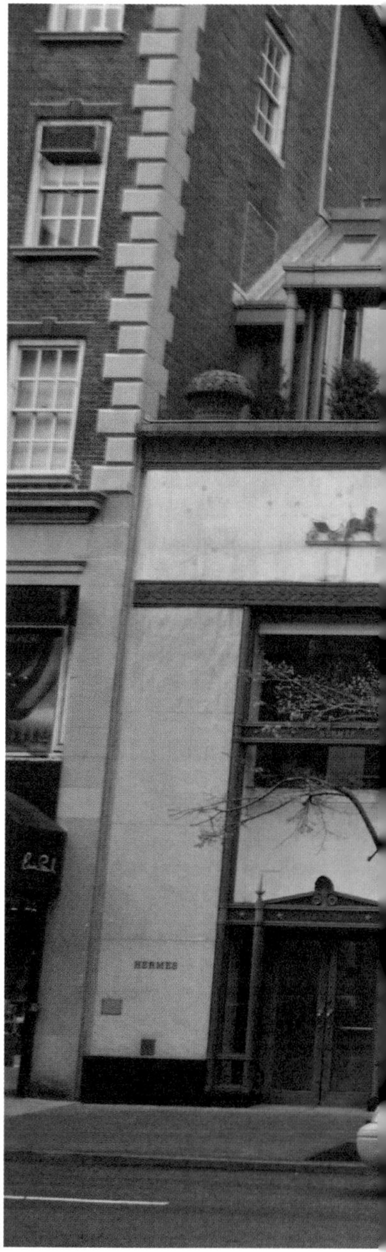

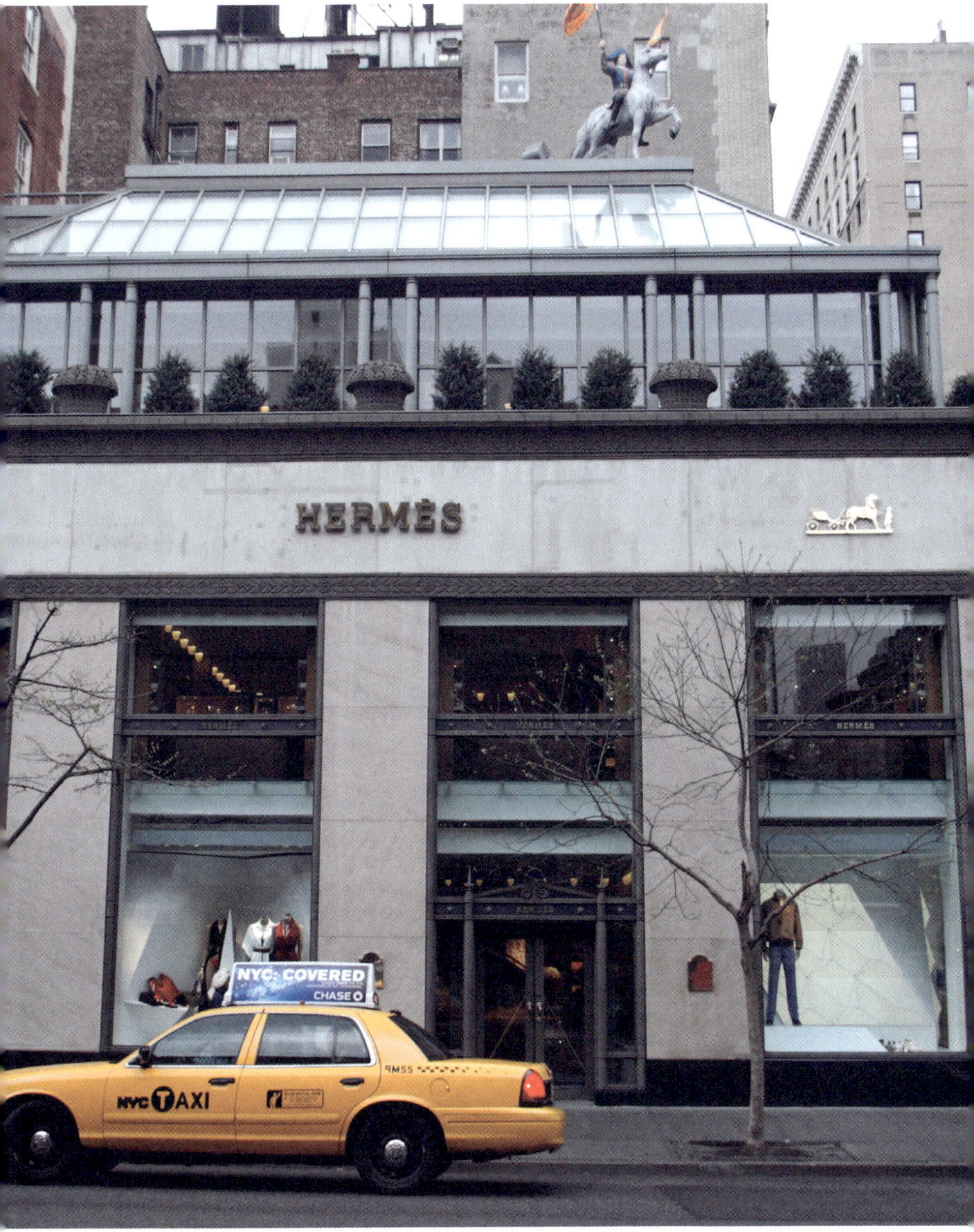
HERMÈS
NYC: COVERED
CHASE
NYC TAXI

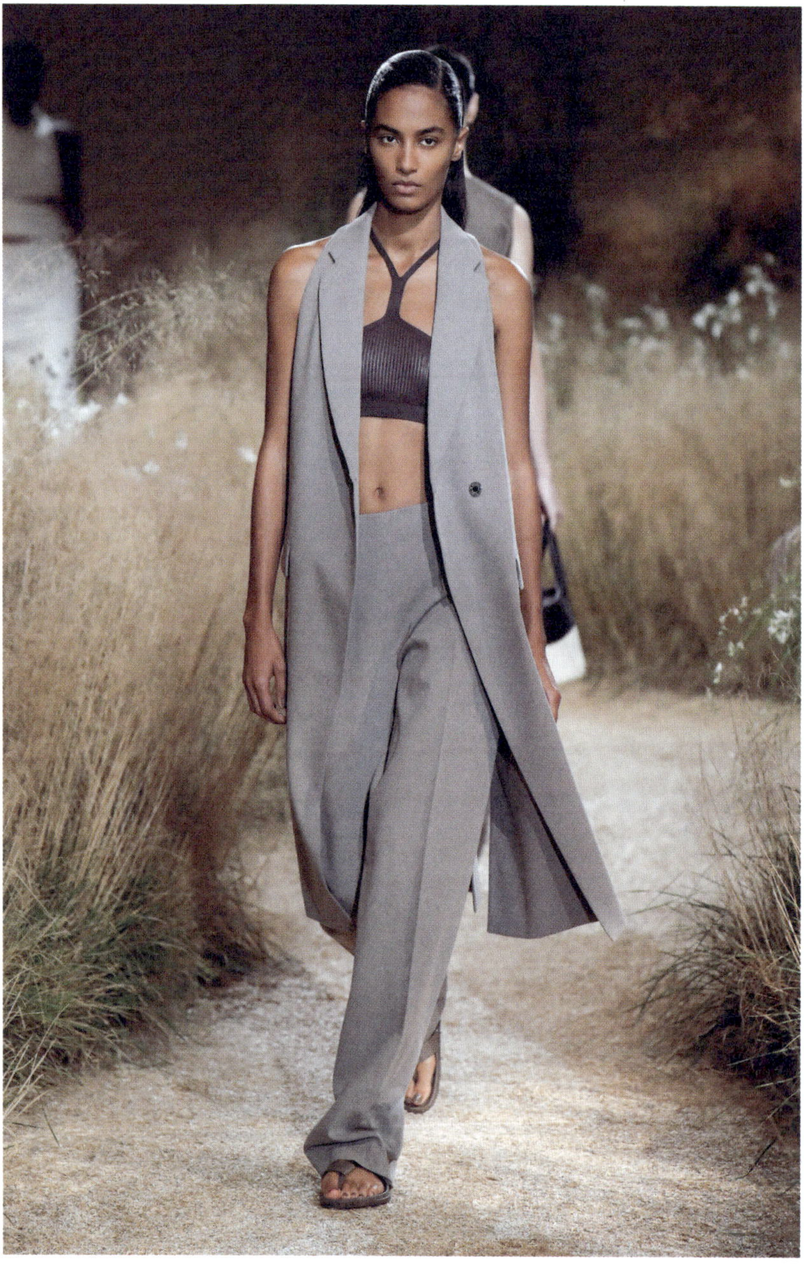

In some fun news for the brand, the colors for spring/summer 2024 that Hermès just released are Orange Field (orange), Gris Misty (gray), and Jaune Milton (cream). Orange Field is meant to be like a meadow of bright poppy flowers. Gris Misty is just a nice bluish-gray that Hermès describes as a "veil of mist." Jaune Milton hasn't been as well received; some say it looks like the color of mayonnaise. Regardless, it's a soft yellowy cream that is a tribute to Milton Clark Avery, an American painter who was known for his soft washes of color on canvas.

Hermès is a luxury brand that cares about the environment and various charitable endeavors. They are committed to humanist values in sustainability, such as making sure that their items don't end up in landfills. In fact, Hermès items are meant to last practically forever. If something is damaged, there are repair shops run by the company that help to restore objects.

This historic brand is committed to using natural resources and are transparent about where the materials they use come from. They strive to control their carbon footprint as a company, making a commitment to preserving biodiversity as one of their pillars of sustainability. It seems like Hermès is well on the way to being a brand that everyone admires for another 200 years.

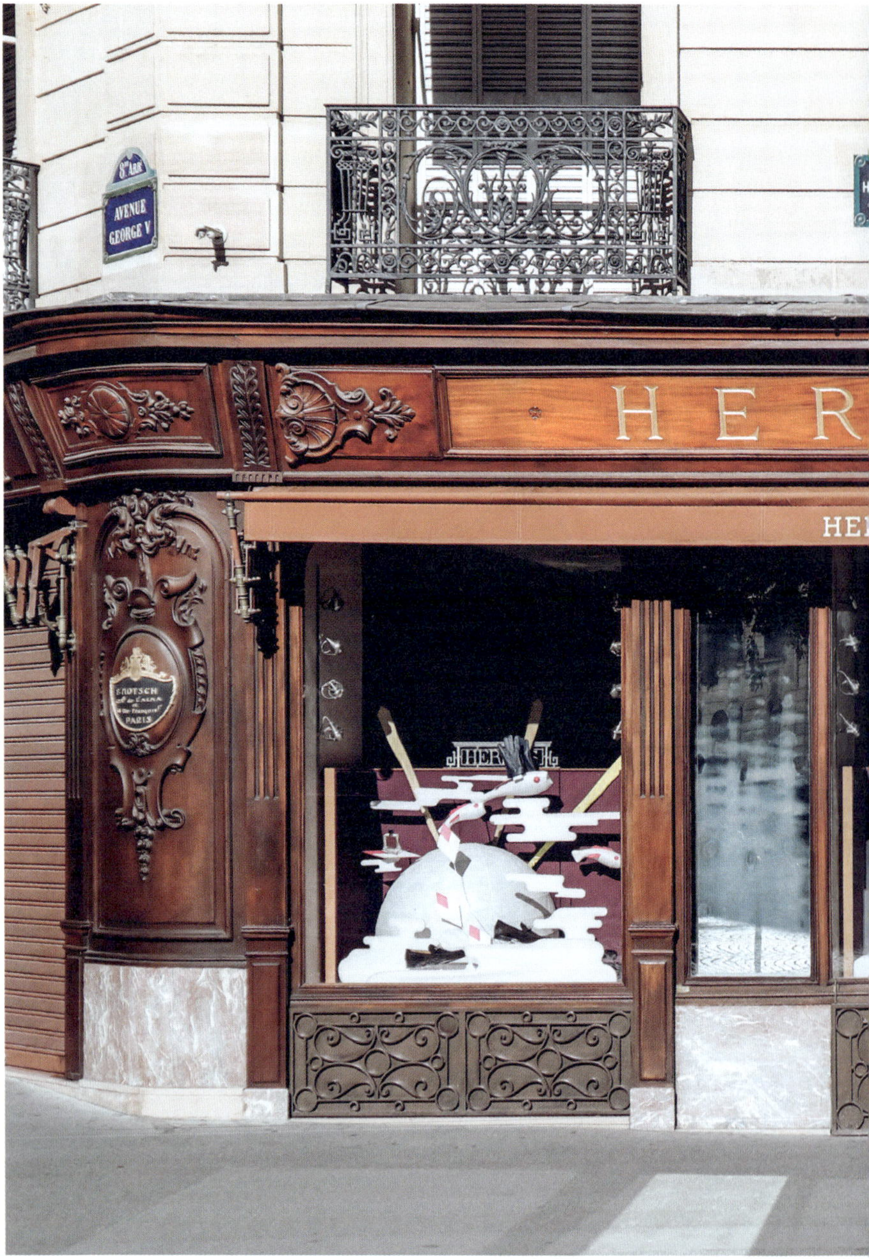
AVENUE
GEORGE V
HER
HER

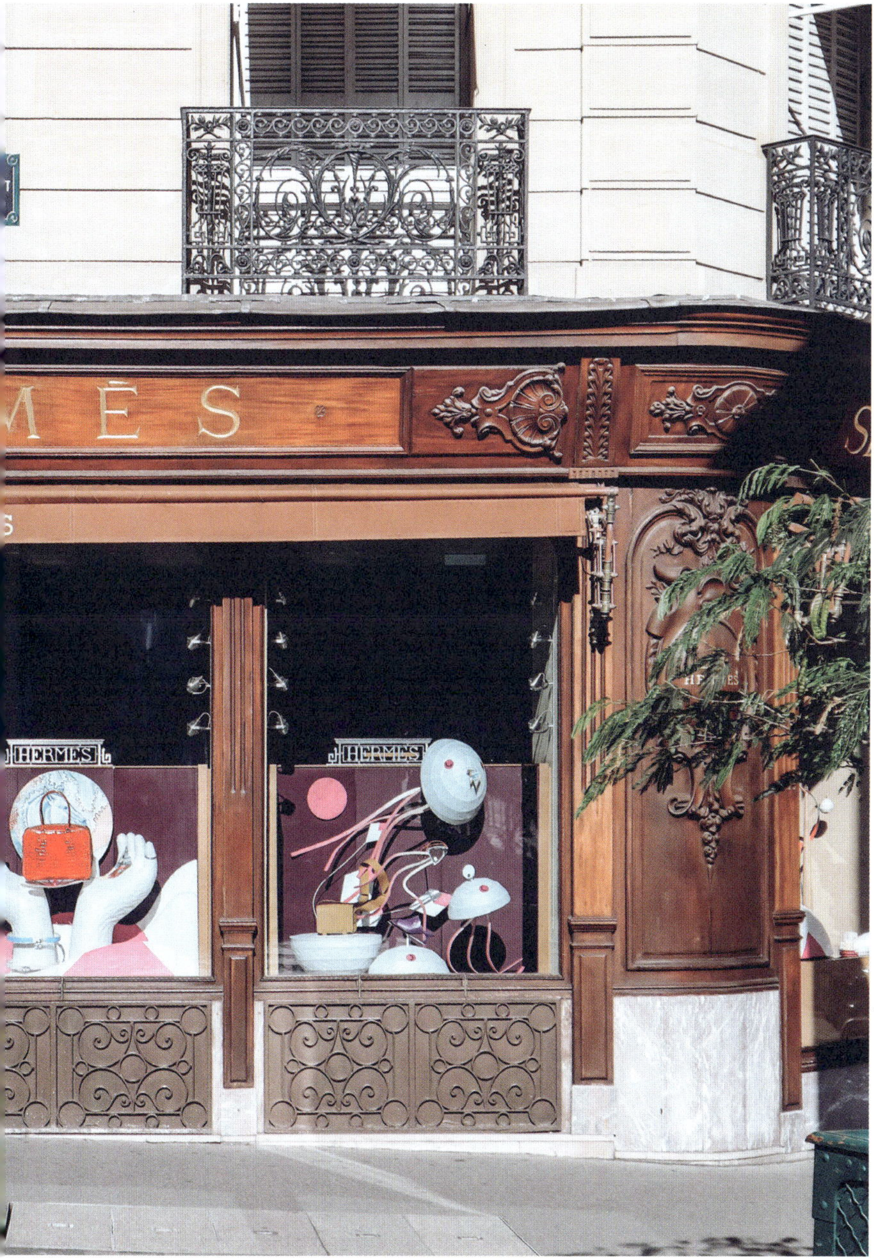
MÈS
HERMÈS
HERMÈS

“I CREATED THE MOST BEAUTI-FUL THINGS IN THE WORLD, BECAUSE THEY’RE USEFUL.”

Thierry Hermès

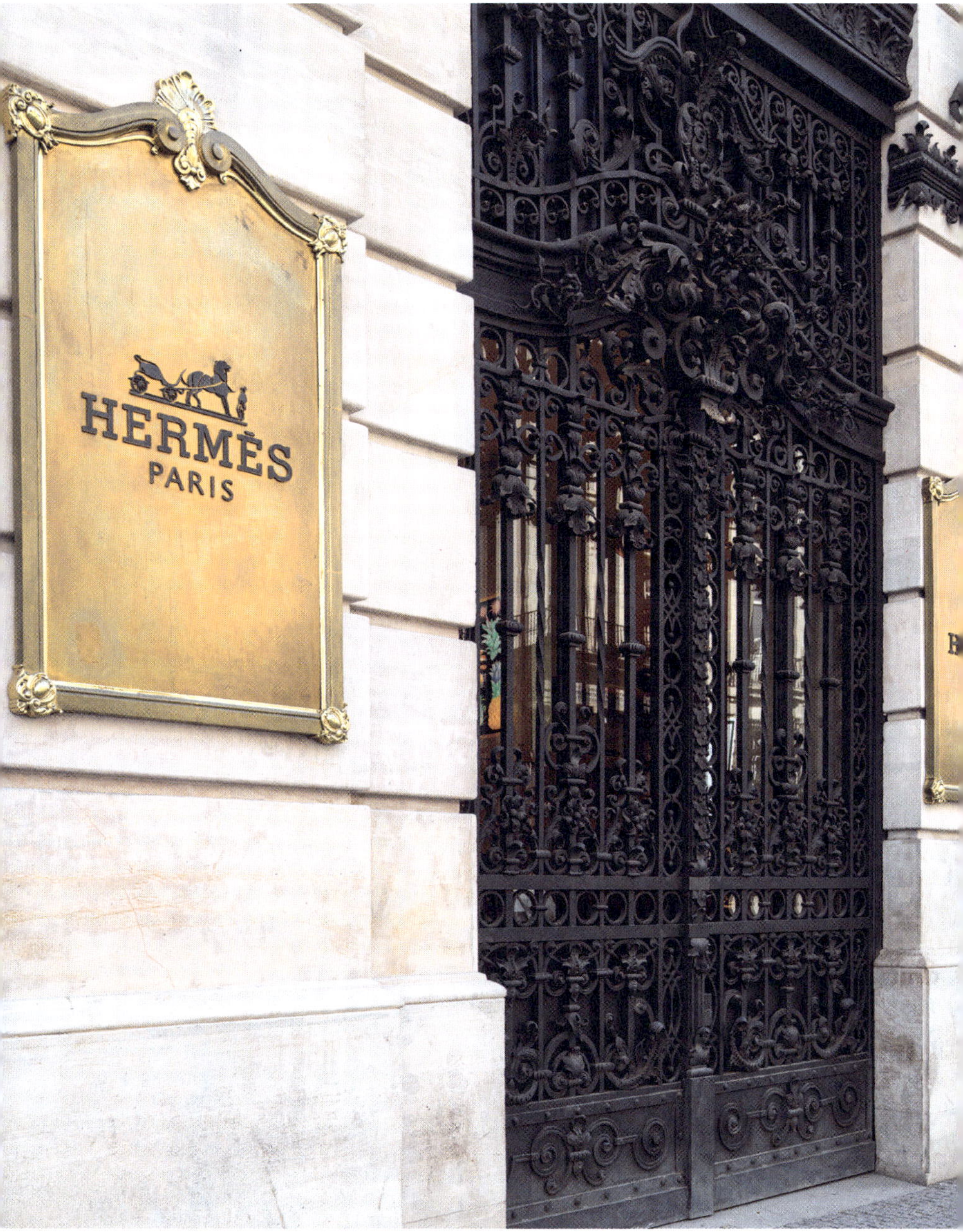
HERMÈS
PARIS

CREDITS

Helmin & Sorgenfri would like to thank the following for permission to use images in this book.

Valentina Linnik		6
Valentina Linnik		7
FarabolaBridgeman Images		8
	chairish.com	8
Valentina Linnik		11
Tea	Dreamstime.com	12/13
Ifeelstock	Dreamstime.com	15
firstVIEW		18
Gavin Zeigler	Alamy Stock Photo	19
Abaca Press	Alamy Stock Photo	21
Abaca Press	Alamy Stock Photo	22
firstVIEW		24
Sipa USA	Alamy Stock Photo	25
firstVIEW		26/27
lev radin	Shutterstock.com	29
GAUTIER Stephane	Alamy Stock Photo	33
614 Collection	Alamy Stock Photo	34
Tatiana Belova	Dreamstime.com	35
Philip Yabut	Shutterstock.com	37
Camera Rules	Shutterstock.com	38
Featureflash	Dreamstime.com	41
newsphoto	Alamy Stock Photo	45
John Muggenborg	Alamy Stock Photo	47
Joli Closet		48
Fortgens Photography	Shutterstock.com	49
Patti McConville	Alamy Stock Photo	50/51
AndiaAlamy	Stock Photo	54/55
STEPHEN FLEMING	Alamy Stock Photo	56
	carredeparis.com	57
AFF	Alamy Stock Photo	59
Jack Skeens	Shutterstock.com	62
Targa56	Shutterstock.com	63
Patti McConville	Alamy Stock Photo	65
Targa56	Shutterstock.com	66
Valentina Linnik		67
Targa56	Shutterstock.com	69
Tinseltown	Shutterstock.com	71
Tatanka005	Shutterstock.com	75
Cristi Dangeorge	Shutterstock.com	76

Trinity MirrorMirrorpix	Alamy Stock Photo	78/79
Cristi Dangeorge	Shutterstock.com	81
photo-lime	Shutterstock.com	82
Abaca Press	Alamy Stock Photo	83
Cristi Dangeorge	Shutterstock.com	83
Sorbis	Shutterstock.com	84/85
photo-lime	Shutterstock.com	87
photo-lime	Shutterstock.com	89
Camera Rules	Shutterstock.com	90
Imaginechina Limited	Alamy Stock Photo	93
Valentina Linnik		97
Sorbis	Shutterstock.com	98
EQRoy	Shutterstock.com	99
Sorbis	Shutterstock.com	100
SEBASTIAN NARITA	Shutterstock.com	102
Ganka Trendafilova	Shutterstock.com	103
Patti McConville	Alamy Stock Photo	104
Patti McConville	Alamy Stock Photo	105
Kathy Hutchins	Shutterstock.com	107
Fabio Diena	Dreamstime.com	111
RiskyWalls	Alamy Stock Photo	112
RiskyWalls	Alamy Stock Photo	113
AGIF	Shutterstock.com	115
Andia	Alamy Stock Photo	119
WENN Rights Ltd	Alamy Stock Photo	120
GTCRFOTO	Alamy Stock Photo	121
INSTAR Images LLC	Alamy Stock Photo	123
INSTAR Images LLC	Alamy Stock Photo	124
WENN Rights Ltd	Alamy Stock Photo	125
WENN Rights Ltd	Alamy Stock Photo	126
WENN Rights Ltd	Alamy Stock Photo	127
s_bukley	Shutterstock.com	128
GTCRFOTO	Alamy Stock Photo	129
Featureflash	Dreamstime.com	131
Maurice Savage	Alamy Stock Photo	135
firstVIEW1		36
Andrei Antipov	stock.adobe.com	138/139
Sergio Delle Vedove	stock.adobe.com	141

Published in 2024 by Helmin & Sorgenfri
Nivå Strandpark 21, 1
DK-2990 Nivå
Denmark

TEXT: Kelly Reising
DESIGN: butter am brot / Morten Svendsen

ISBN: 978-87-94190-61-9

Printed in EU
1. edition, 1. printing

MIX
Paper | Supporting responsible forestry
FSC® C118234
FSC www.fsc.org